Miles —
  Here's something
to read at
bedtime or any-
time
  I Love You,
      Mommy

# LITTLE BOOK OF

# STEAM

Clive Groome

LITTLE BOOK OF
# STEAM

First published in the UK in 2007

© G2 Entertainment Limited 2011

www.G2ent.co.uk

Printed and bound printed in the EU

ISBN 978-1-907803-10-9

# Contents

# Foreword

CLIVE GROOME IS A MAN who warms my heart. He is an Engineman and he is a real Railwayman which is a compliment that had to be earned. He joined the Southern Region of BR at Norwood Junction shed in 1951 at the age of 15 and a year later, he was firing now and again on the W tanks to Willesden, Ferme Park and Old Oak and even on the K class Moguls to Brighton. But he craved for the big time and in 1954 he went to Nine Elms as a fireman in the Tank Gang and some good training, for the old 'soft-beat' M7s were not easy engines. Soon after, he was called up for National Service in the RASC and when he returned, he was in the 'Tavy' gang with Jim Dawson and the old Urie 'Chonkers' on heavy, fast freight work. He loved those "H15"s, never fast but mighty strong and he was learning all the time from Jim who gave him a wonderful grounding in the art of firing. Promotion was fast and after a few months, he was moved up to No 2 with Driver Len Rickard, another splendid mate who enjoyed firing and had sufficient confidence in Clive to give him the opportunity of some priceless driving experience both on the Salisbury and the Bournemouth roads.

Indeed it was said that anybody who had fired for both Dawson and Rickard had the makings of an engineman and was sure to pass the test which Clive did when he was 23. Once he was passed he got plenty of driving at a time when young men were at last being used on fast train work at Nine Elms and until the end of steam in 1967, he loved the work which meant everything to him. But the diesels and electrics were a different matter and, by 1979, he left the railway to study for a degree in Social Sciences. He had also written an excellent article for The Guardian about the lot of an electric train driver which brought him some useful publicity on both TV and Radio but railways were in his blood and in 1985, he was able to set up a training programme in footplate skills at Sheffield Park for

budding footplate staff on some of the preserved railways. And now he is a legendary figure, a man who can instruct, amuse and absorb and who has a devoted circle of friends to whom he has given so much. But there is more to come, a breadth of vision. When he was on leave in the RASC, he used it to ride with Bill Hoole on the A4s out of Kings Cross and, in later years, on my engines out of Liverpool Street. It was a joy to help such a man for one knew that not only was he gaining experience but, above all, he was adding to his knowledge and the understanding of human nature which counts for so much in railway life and in his work today. Indeed, I wish he had chosen to come to Stewarts Lane when I was there in 1954 rather than along the road at Nine Elms!

*Mr R H N Hardy C Eng, FI Mech E.*
*Writer and Lecturer.*
*Shedmaster of Stewarts Lane*
*(Southern Region) August 1952 to*
*January 1955.*
*District Motive Power Superintendent*
*Liverpool Street January 1959 to*
*December 1962.*

OPPOSITE Clive Groome on the set of the remake of 'The Railway Children'

# Introduction

TWENTY-ONE YEARS AFTER Trevithick had first demonstrated that self-propelled steam engines could haul colliery wagons better than horses, the first public railway, the Stockton and Darlington, commenced operation. A machine which resembled a large iron grasshopper on wheels attracted the awe and attention of the local populace. Like the horses that still laboured in the service of Mankind the strange machine had a body heat that could be felt as the onlookers approached with wary steps. It smelled of hot iron and warm oil and above its tall chimney the air shimmered, enlivened by the rising gases from its furnace. Its attendant driver and grimy fireman performed arcane and unfamiliar acts standing aloof from the crowd on the small footplating fixed to the machine's barrel, and lo, the machine's metal limbs twitched and its breath came in gasps as it lurched into movement. With no horse in the shafts and dripping water that fizzed and spat at the flinching yet delighted audience, it slowly rolled forward, creaking, squeaking, its iron wheels bearing down on iron rails.

A hundred and eighty years later the driver of any steam locomotive will find himself and his machine to be the object of intense interest. Delight will shine in the eyes of young children as they mimic with their arms the rise and fall of the coupling rods, or whoop in imitation of the engines whistle as it runs into the station. Quite clearly this machine has enduring charisma. We who are privileged to operate them are no less entranced by the need to learn and practice the art of managing their power, and are no less aware of the beauty of their varied shapes and distinctive "voices".

pumping engines of Newcomen and Watt its main topic will be the railway steam locomotives that were made possible by the raising of working pressures and consequent miniaturisation of engines (a locomotive has at least two "engines"). Locomotive is a long and sometimes cumbersome word, so I will often refer to them as engines instead. Today it is common for the

**LEFT** The opening of the Stockton and Darlington, the first ever public railway, in 1825

**BELOW** It may not look much, but this was the first steam-powered railway engine

Today when most of us find that computers have taken the satisfaction out of performing almost all jobs, be they administrative or manual, eight hundred people a year ask me to teach them to drive a steam engine. Men (and women) of all ages and from around the world have applied themselves to the hard and dirty work of managing a steam locomotive to a safe and efficient standard under close supervision. In some cases an introductory session sets them off on the long (ten-year) road to qualifying as a driver on a preserved line. For the majority a one-day session fulfils a dream that was unrealised but ever present since childhood.

Although this Little Book of Steam starts out with the large stationary

public to ask me which 'train' they will drive when they mean which engine. I suppose the multiple unit diesel or electric sets that make up the modern train may have blurred the distinction between the conveyance and the power source for the average passenger.

This study, however brief and within a little book, of the development of the steam locomotive over a two hundred year period will explain "why engines look the way they do". It will offer a general description of the way they work and of how the men that developed them came together then branched out on their individual paths of creative effort.

The overall "dish" will be flavoured by the "spice" that is unavoidable if the "cook" happens to be a professional operator of the machine in question and has done so for the major part of his adult life. This old engineman had a "revelation" the other day when he stood on the footplate of the re-created broad gauge engine Firefly at the Didcot Railway Centre. I was in the company of driver Peter Jennings and fireman, and chairman of the Firefly group, Sam Bee. The revelation went like this: I was standing on the footplate of a small 2-2-2 tender locomotive, the size of the single driving wheel was about seven feet. Its splasher had openings through which the wheel spokes were visible and I was prevented from falling off the footplate by low ornamental railings, much like those that can sometimes be found surrounding a bed of flowers, and I was reminded of an early paddle steamer. In front of me I found no spectacle plate, no windows through which to look and hence no cab or cab roof! And yet Sam informed me that this class of locomotive regularly ran trains to Paddington from Westbury at speeds of up to sixty miles per hour, in all weathers and by night and day.

Now, I know what this means, because I have driven old tender locomotives in reverse at almost the same speed. In the winter it is horrible and painful to the ears, the eyes and the jaw! And we had a cab and cab roof around us. For the first time I saluted the courage and strength of the men that did their work with less than a garden gate between them and being cast overboard at speed. Between them and the elements that struck at them from all sides while one shovelled and the other peered, watery eyed, looking for dim oil lamps that signalled yay or nay to their onward rush. And the brakes were yet to be made perfect, and they did eighteen hour days very often because "one man one engine" was the rule and they would have hated another man's hand to operate "their" engine.

So for the first time I appreciated the courage of these old timers who were the "astronauts" of their age. Now the early history of the steam engine came to life and I looked anew at the old prints and plans of Stephenson's, Gooch's and Crampton's machines. Dry historical facts are enlivened. The early

BELOW Engine drivers were proud of their job and this one has a young enthusiast in the cab

days, made tedious by endless repetition in text books, are, to this engine-driving man at least, now full of human endeavour and stoicism. As the story unfolds we must imagine these 'old timers' regaling newcomers to their craft with tales of derring do (we still do this to newcomers to the footplate). The hours on duty had to be reduced before the sleep inducing over all cabs could be introduced in Britain. Improvements in steel led to faster speeds. Improvements to pay led to larger engines, therefore higher productivity from less engines per train and less engine crews to work them.

Enginemen were seldom as scruffy as the average film director or costume manager dictates to the professional "stunt driver" of steam locomotives today! Please note... enginemen were generally the dandies of the manual workers, "silk hatted aristocrats of the line" wrote someone. Main line drivers and firemen wore collars and ties. Drivers had polished shoes. Overalls were sometimes starched by mother at home. One has only to look at the old prints of enginemen and early photographs to see the pride taken in the turnout of the locomotive and its crew.

The locomotives of Britain were exported and adapted to the rougher conditions prevailing in the USA and elsewhere. Many of the adaptations came back to the home country and carried forward the improvements into British practice. Particularly in the case of the GWR which became American/French in order to create the best boiler and engine layout of the day.

Experimental designs are hard to justify to those that have to pay for them and perhaps lose the prospect of dividends if a mistake is made by the Chief Mechanical Engineer. Following America's lead, simplicity of maintenance and cheapness of construction eventually became the order of the day in the final sad days of main line British steam.

But, as in all good stories, the hero - defeated, succumbs only to bound back reinvigorated - in our case by the undiminished desire of laymen and some stubborn railwaymen to see and operate their beloved steam locomotives again. We have today several hundred examples of the old machines still operating, with

ABOVE Every schoolboy wanted to be an engine driver!

a small number of completely new machines outshopped or in progress.

When you read this account of the history of steam you will find many omissions from the full story. Please forgive me. In compensation I have given an insiders view that may help you to understand the human side of those events. Throughout my research and throughout my career one wonderful fact keeps emerging: the love that Mankind had and still has for this machine. From the cleaner to the shedmaster. The spotter to the railway doyen. The apprentice to the Chief Mechanical Engineer. The history of steam is also the history of those who spent their lives in its thrall.

It is a familiar yet inspiring story we offer in this Little Book of Steam.

# Chapter 1

# Early Pioneers

BY THE END OF THE EIGHTEENTH century the creations of Newcomen and Watt had brought to light the power available for the use of Mankind by the harnessing of steam. Some two hundred and fifty years later we in our nuclear age may easily forget that the power we rely on today still depends on water turned into steam, which is then used to make electricity. Miniaturisation may be a modern buzzword but this is essentially what first William Murdoch and later Richard Trevithick achieved just before the turn of the nineteenth century. They discovered that engines could be made much smaller if the pressure of the steam used to drive them was increased, and it eventually occurred to both men that it might be possible to put such an engine onto wheels. In 1784 Murdoch built a three wheeled model powered by a spirit lamp that he tested one Sunday evening near his home at Redruth. The little model hissed and spat furiously as it twisted and turned about, its trial run successful enough to be the source of some consternation to the local congregation, many of whom were convinced they were being confronted by a manifestation of the devil as they left the church. Trevithick made a full size road vehicle in 1802 and, together with his assistant Andrew Vivian, drove it from Redruth to Plymouth, then shipped it to London for further demonstration.

After suffering a couple of setbacks he lost interest in the project and turned to rail mounted engines. Two years later at Pen-y-darren in South Wales, he produced a travelling engine that was to be the world's first steam railway locomotive. The engine was notable for the fact that it ran on smooth flangeless wheels within smooth flanged iron plates demonstrating that given sufficient weight the wheels would maintain their grip under power. Unfortunately however, this weight was too much for the iron plates designed for horse-drawn traffic, and many of them broke under the strain. Despite this hazard, Trevithick's engine hauled a ten ton load more than nine miles, the journey taking four hours to complete. As the engine had only one piston it would have been necessary to push or lever it into motion should the piston have stopped at either extremity of its travel. Also, as there was no means of admitting water to the boiler the entire run had to completed on a single filling - fortunately the steam pressure was low.

The advantage of making smooth surfaces over which to run horse-drawn wagons had been discovered in antiquity. Instead of creating full blown Roman road surfaces a couple of strips of hard wood were found to be sufficient to ease the passage of wheels over soft ground, and the continuation of this process lead to the creation of 'plateways'. At Pen-y-darren these wooden plateways had been replaced by flanged iron plates in common with many colliery railways at the time. When it was later found that the flanged plates collected rubbish they were discarded in favour of edge rails on which flanged wheels could run and take guidance on curves with minimal friction. Gradients too steep for horses were surmounted by rope haulage from fixed engine houses. For the really steep gradients at the Middleton Colliery owned by John Blenkinsop, Leeds engineer Matthew Murray in 1812 built a steam engine driven by a toothed wheel

OPPOSITE William Murdoch worked out that steam engines could be smaller if the pressure was increased

BELOW Richard Trevithick was one of the pioneers of steam locomotion

ABOVE William
Murdoch's early model
steam engine with
three wheels

OPPOSITE Steam
Engine pioneer George
Stephenson examining
'Puffing Billy' built by
William Hedley

set one crank at ninety degrees to the other, thus avoiding 'centring' on a dead spot. A year later at Wylam Colliery, William Hedley demonstrated that a rack was unnecessary when by experimentation he discovered the precise amount of adhesive weight needed for a given load. His engine had a U shaped flue tube that ran most of the length of the boiler, the chimney being the same end of the boiler as the fire grate, thus providing the boiler with a larger heating surface. The exhaust pipe from the cylinders was inserted into the chimney stack, softening the harshness of the blast (which had frightened horses) and the engine became known as 'Puffing Billy'. However, Hedley had still not solved the problem of the fragile plateways, and eventually Puffing Billy's unsprung weight proved to be such a nuisance that for a time the engine was converted to run on eight wheels to spread the load. Later the plateway

engaging in a rack cast integrally with the rails. The engine was constructed with minimum weight, and thus minimal adhesion, to avoid the problems with the brittle iron plateway. The rack gear provided the locomotive with the traction necessary to climb the colliery gradients. In order to make an engine that would start on a hill without needing to be pushed or levered into action, Murray fitted not one but two steam cylinders and was taken up and replaced by rails which were more able to support the weight of the engine, and in 1830 Puffing Billy was reconverted to her original four wheel configuration. Subsequently this engine worked on the Wylam Colliery until 1862 when a change of gauge finally forced her retirement. However, Puffing Billy was preserved and can still be seen today on display in the London Science Museum.

None of the engines described so far had springs. This was because engines with vertical cylinders or which were driven by gears had to maintain a fixed relationship between axle centre and boiler centre. Any springing would cause disengagement of gearing or alter the clearances of the piston and cylinder end covers.

At Killingworth Colliery enginewright George Stephenson was earning himself a good reputation as a 'fixer' of sick engines. His father had been an engineman at the mine and at an early age George had taken a great interest in the pumping engines and the way they were made. His cleverness at engine 'doctoring' later made him famous and wealthy enough to provide

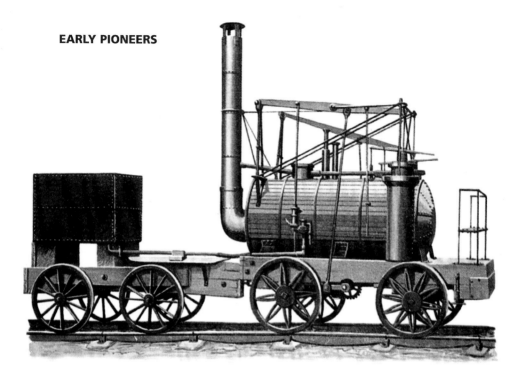

his own son Robert with an excellent
education that he himself had never
had. The success of Hedley's engine at
nearby Wylam Colliery prompted
George's employers to ask him to build
a similar engine for Killingworth. After
some study of Hedley's engine, George
began to construct a version with his
own improvements to the valve gear,
and with the two cylinders half set
into the boiler barrel. This engine was
completed in 1814. As in Hedley's
engine the power was transmitted by
gear wheels which ensured the cranks
remained at right angles to each other.
When the gears became worn out,
George was instructed to build a second engine and this time he attached

the connecting rods directly to the crank pins on the wheels. In order to prevent one wheelset slipping and altering the ninety degree setting the wheelsets were coupled together by rods between the frames fitted to cranked axles. However, the cranked axles were weak and the next engine Stephenson built in 1816 had a cog on each axle connected by a continuous chain which served to maintain the ninety degree relationship without weakening the axle. This engine was also fitted with steam springing. In both engines the exhaust steam was passed into the chimney, and their wheels were flanged. A further six engines of a similar type were built by George Stephenson between 1816 and 1822 before he began work on Locomotion.

The engines so far described were all working in the enclosed confines of the colliery for which they were built, they were not used for public haulage.

BELOW George Stephension refined the Puffing Billy concept for Killingworth Colliery

# Chapter 2

# Steam Goes Public

THE SUCCESS ENJOYED BY Stephenson's engines while shifting coal became widely known and Stephenson was soon asked by other colliery owners to build engines for them. In 1822 he completed an 8 mile line from the Hetton Colliery near Sunderland to the docks on the banks of the Wear. The steeper gradients of this line were worked by stationary engines and cables, but the more level sections were worked by steam locomotives built by himself to a design similar to the engines in use at Killingworth, with the chain coupled wheels. This experience was no doubt of great benefit to Stephenson when he became involved in a far more ambitious project. Incorporated by Act of Parliament in 1821, the Stockton and Darlington Railway was a public company, financed by public investors with the aim of building a public railway from the Durham coal fields around Darlington to the important port of Stockton-on-Tees. It was initially proposed that all traffic would be horse-drawn, but one of the major stockholders, a Quaker named Edward Pease, was persuaded by Stephenson that the freight traffic at least should be hauled by steam locomotives. Eventually after some wrangling, Stephenson was assigned the post of engineer, responsible for building the line and providing the steam locomotives to work the freight traffic. This appointment was to prove more costly to the board of the S & D than they had originally anticipated. The first thing Stephenson stipulated was that he did not want to use the brittle cast iron fishbelly plates normally used on the colliery plateways. Wrought or rolled iron rails such as those patented by John Birkinshaw of the Bedlington Iron Works in 1820 were far more durable and were easily able to support the weight of any present or future locomotive that Stephenson might build to work the railway. Unfortunately they were also double the cost, but with a little persuasion and with the backing of Edward Pease, Stephenson eventually got his way. He also secured an order for three locomotives to work the line. Stephenson had initially decided to build the Stockton and Darlington Railway to a gauge of four feet eight inches, but he soon discovered that an extra half inch distance between the rails did much to reduce friction without any detriment to the security of the locomotives and rolling stock. 'Standard gauge' was born.

On Tuesday, 27th September 1825 the Stockton and Darlington Railway opened for business, the inaugural train being hauled by engine No 1, Locomotion, the first of the three steam locomotives George Stephenson had contracted to build for the new railway. Despite the fact that it had been agreed that all passenger traffic would be horse-drawn, a passenger coach of sorts had been built and was sandwiched in the middle of the train of more than thirty wagons of coal. Important dignitaries sat in the coach while every one else scrambled for any place they could get onto each of the coal wagons. Eventually everyone was in place and Locomotion began to wheeze her way forward. She succeeded in hauling the ninety ton train the length of the line at a reasonably constant speed of between twelve and fifteen miles per hour, much to the satisfaction of all on board. Especially to the dignitaries in the coach, who for the very first time began to see that there might be some possibility of a return

BELOW Robert Stephenson, George's only son, worked closely with his father

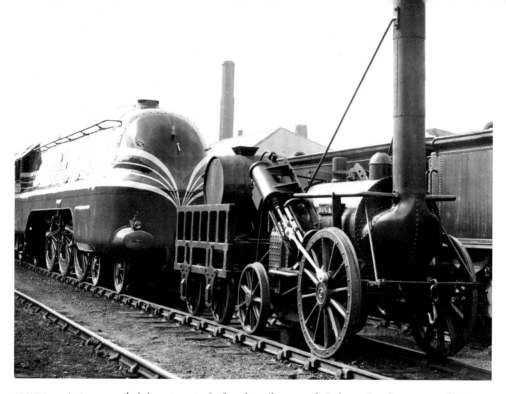

on their investments. In fact the railway was so successful that by the end of November the cost of transporting coal had been so reduced that the price of coal in Stockton had fallen by a third, eighteen months later it had been halved and the railway was already beginning to return a profit.

Locomotion was the first locomotive to be built in the new workshops of Robert Stephenson and Co At around 8 tons in weight, she had a single flue boiler with a working pressure of 25lb psi and two vertical cylinders each driving a pair of cast iron wheels four feet in diameter. The cylinders were connected directly to the driving wheels which were coupled either side of the engine with horizontal rods. The cranks were set ninety degrees to

**ABOVE** Locomotion, the first locomotive to be built in the new workshops of Robert Stephenson and Co, in 1825

each other so that each cylinder was set to give its maximum output in turn with the other, thus minimising starting problems and enabling the engine to haul a train at a constant rate. The design was well suited for slow and heavy work, such as hauling many wagons of coal, but was inadequate for travel at any constant speed above 16 mph. Due to the single flue boiler the engine would simply run out of steam if too much was asked of it. However, George and Robert Stephenson were well aware of Locomotion's shortcomings and although they built three more like her for the coal trains of the Stockton and Darlington, they had something else in mind for faster trains of the future.

# Chapter 3

# The Rainhill Trials

THE STOCKTON AND DARLINGTON was an unqualified success. Although all passenger traffic was initially drawn by horses, it was not long before someone had the idea of running mixed trains which were inevitably followed by passenger only trains hauled by faster engines. Not everybody was happy with this situation, however, and when George Stephenson declared that he could build an engine capable of a constant speed of twenty miles per hour a horrified member of the public wrote to the Quarterly Review: "What can be palpably more absurd and ridiculous, than the prospect held out of locomotives travelling twice as fast as stagecoaches? We would as soon expect the people of Woolwich to suffer

themselves to be fired off in one of Congreve's ricochet-rockets, as trust themselves to the mercy of such a machine going at such a rate." No doubt reports from recent wars were fresh in the author's mind, the highly dangerous but very effective rockets designed by Sir William Congreve in 1805 and used by the British against both the French and the Americans having made a name for themselves in a typically spectacular fashion. As a matter of interest, George Stephenson had himself been drafted to fight in the Napoleonic wars but he paid another man to go in his place. It is fortunate indeed that he did so, otherwise it would have been many years before he could have returned to England to con-

tinue with his development of the steam engine and he might well have been killed.

For some time it had been proposed to build a railway connecting the cities of Liverpool and Manchester and, despite the best efforts of landowners, horse breeders and coachmen, the necessary bill was eventually passed through Parliament. George Stephenson was appointed

constructing engineer responsible for the survey, design and execution of the civil engineering works required to build the railway. This entailed several particularly difficult works to overcome various natural features including a "floating" embankment across Chat Moss, twelve square miles of peat bog, a two mile cutting at Olive Mount, a one and a half mile tunnel from Liverpool Station to Edgehill and the nine arch Sankey Viaduct. Naturally Stephenson was insistent that the line should be worked by steam engines, but the Liverpool and Manchester board of directors were not so sure. Many were still in favour of the more traditional methods of traction, either by horses or by cables powered by stationary engines. Fortunately this last option was projected to be extremely expensive, as it had been calculated that some twenty one stationary steam engines would have been required to work the traffic the full length of the line. After much lengthy and sometimes acrimonious debate the board eventually agreed to give the 'travelling engine' a chance. It was decided that a prize of £500 would be awarded to the best engine built within certain specifications, that ran economically and performed well according

OPPOSITE Critics compared the thought of riding at 20mph to being fired from one of Sir William Congreve's rockets!

to certain set parameters as defined by the board.

George Stephenson had by now left the design and building of locomotive engines to his son, Robert, and his company Robert Stephenson and Co His last effort had been the aptly named Experiment, an engine which he built in 1827 for the Stockton and Darlington Railway, and which had two flues in the boiler thus doubling the overall heating surface. Although the idea was later abandoned as boiler maintenance proved to be too complicated, Experiment had proved the benefits of the increased heating area. In 1828

Robert Stephenson built a four wheeled engine called Lancashire Witch for the Bolton and Leigh Railway. Instead of the normal vertical cylinders, this engine was the first to have her cylinders inclined and mounted at the rear of the boiler, directly driving the front two wheels. This arrangement allowed the axles of the locomotive to be properly sprung for the first time. The locomotive Robert Stephenson built for the Rainhill Trials was the culmination of these designs but had one very important additional feature. As the result of a suggestion by Henry Booth, the secretary of the Liverpool and Manchester Railway, the

engine was built with a boiler incorporating twenty-five three-inch copper tubes which considerably increased its heating capacity. At six feet long and with a working pressure of 50lbs psi, the boiler was the first to have a proper firebox at the rear. The inclined cylinders were mounted either side of the firebox and drove the front pair of single driving wheels directly via connecting rod and crankpin. The exhaust from each cylinder was directed up the chimney via blast pipes carefully tapered to provide the optimum draw on the fire. The entire locomotive weighed less than four and a half tons, not an awful lot more than the tender that was attached to it which weighed over three tons when fully laden with water and coal. The engine proved to be capable of sustained speeds of up to thirty miles an hour and was duly christened Rocket, partly, no doubt, as a tribute to her fleet-footedness, but possibly also as an unabashed gesture to all those who doubted that such a machine was either safe or desirable.

There were many prospective entries to the Liverpool and Manchester's contest, some less sensible than others. These were gradually weeded out until eventually there were only four contenders for the prize other than Rocket. One was a four wheeled locomotive named Sanspareil entered by Timothy Hackworth, another was the appropriately named Novelty, a highly unusual four wheeled engine entered by John Braithwaite and Captain John Ericsson, a Swede. A third engine named Perseverance, also had four wheels and was the entry of a Scot named Timothy Burstall. The only other suitable contestant was Edward Bury of Liverpool, and although he was not able to complete his engine in time for the trials he was later to make significant contributions towards the evolution of the steam engine.

Hackworth had previously worked for George Stephenson and at the time of the contest was the locomotive superintendent of the Stockton and Darlington Railway. He was noted for his rebuilding of an engine that had been given the disparaging nickname of Chittaprat because of the terrible noise it made. Supplied by a Newcastle firm for the Stockton and Darlington Railway, No 5

had four cylinders and four driving wheels, with a pair of cylinders each driving a separate pair of driving wheels without any coupling between the two. The engine had not been a success and when it was damaged in an accident, Hackworth took the opportunity to scrap it and make use of its boiler. The result was Royal George, a six coupled engine capable of hauling thirty two wagons of coal weighing around a hundred and thirty tons at a constant speed of five miles an hour, and was at the time one of the most powerful locomotives ever built. Sanspareil was virtually a shortened four wheel version of Royal

George, she had the same 'U' tube boiler and a pair of vertical cylinders mounted over the rear axle. However, she weighed more than five hundredweight over the stipulated maximum and was disqualified although she was later allowed to take part in the trials. By contrast Novelty, the engine of Braithwaite and Ericsson, seemed lightly built, almost elegant in appearance. She easily attained the fastest speed of all the contestants and was a great favourite with the crowd of spectators. Built with an ingenious combined vertical and horizontal boiler feeding a pair of vertical cylinders, Novelty was the only

**CENTRE** Scotsman
Timothy Burstall's
Perseverance only
reached a speed of 6mph

locomotive in the trials to carry her own coal and water supply and has since been regarded as the first tank engine. Burstall's engine, Perseverance, had a vertical boiler mounted on a platform over two pairs of driving wheels, but she was unable to attain the required speed and was withdrawn from the contest.

The Rainhill Trials began on 8th October 1829, and were conducted over a seven day period on the Rainhill Level, a stretch of track less than two miles long near the Liverpool end of the Liverpool and Manchester Railway. A grandstand had been built at the mid point of the track and on the first day some 15,000 people turned up to watch the spectacle. Each contestant was required to complete two runs of thirty-seven and a half miles each, which represented a return trip of the length of the Liverpool and Manchester line. This meant that each engine had to make many journeys up and down the track while attached to a suitable load. One of the requirements made by the Liverpool and Manchester board was that each locomotive should 'consume its own smoke', as they were anxious about the nuisance that might be created by engines belching thick black clouds of soot and ashes. At the trial each

of the contestants burned coke to get around this problem. Both Rocket and Sanspareil used blast pipes that directed exhaust steam from the cylinders up the chimney to draw the fire. Sanspareil's blast pipe was a little severe and was prone to sending a large part of the contents of her fire-flue straight up her chimney, much to the consternation of anyone who happened to be standing nearby. Novelty's fire was drawn not by the exhaust blast but by a set of bellows which

awarded the £500 prize, but also an order for a further seven locomotives similar to Rocket to work the Liverpool and Manchester Railway. It is interesting to note, however, that according to The Liverpool Mercury of October 1829 Rocket was an "old-fashioned locomotive engine" and that the engine entered by Messrs Braithwaite and Ericsson was a "decided improvement in the arrangement, the safety, simplicity, and the smoothness and steadiness of a locomotive engine". The Mercury further reported that but for an unfortunate break down Novelty would have been a clear winner, and that it was the opinion of the general public and "nine-tenths of the engineers and scientific men now in Liverpool" that the principle and construction of all future locomotives would follow her design. Of course the real secret of Rocket's success was hidden from public view, her firebox and multi-tube boiler were a major break through in locomotive design and the foundation of what would become standard practice in the construction of steam engines. Thus, the Stephensons' innovative design and superb workmanship had won the day at Rainhill, and had secured the future of steam traction on the railways.

failed during one of her runs leaving the unfortunate engine unable to make steam. During the many journeys back and forth both Sanspareil and Novelty were beset by various problems until eventually Novelty's boiler failed, as did the boiler feed water pump on Sanspareil, leaving both engines unable to continue. Only Rocket met the board's stringent requirements including running reliably for the entire distance while hauling a load. The Stephensons were not only

# Chapter 4

# Robert Stephenson and Co

THE BUSINESS OF ROBERT STEPHENSON and Company was formed in 1823 by a partnership between George and Robert Stephenson and Edward Pease, the latter providing much of the financial backing. Land was purchased in Forth Street, Newcastle-on-Tyne and a factory built with the particular purpose of steam locomotive construction in mind. It was a bold move at the time because many people, including those who were later to become railway shareholders and board members, were not entirely convinced that steam was a good thing. There were landowners that did not want to see railways 'ruining' the countryside, coach proprietors and horse breeders who were concerned that their business might suffer, and there were those who thought that to travel at speeds in excess of twenty miles an hour was a sin against Nature, and that steam engines were just plain dangerous. If the dissenters had had their way the operating life of Robert Stephenson and Co would have been extremely short.

The new company received its first order for two steam locomotives from the board of the Stockton and Darlington Railway in 1824 but only the first of them, Locomotion, had been completed by the time the Stockton and Darlington opened in 1825. Robert Stephenson, though only twenty years of age, had in 1824 accepted a post with a mining company in South America,

which is where he spent the next three years. George Stephenson found himself caught up in the almost manic desire for railways that had spread country-wide, and in 1824 he was consultant to no less than four separate railway companies, including the Liverpool and Manchester. Accordingly, the new locomotive works in Forth Street had

become a little neglected and Edward Pease began to wonder at the wisdom of his investment. However, George carried on while Robert was abroad, and the orders were slowly fulfilled. He completed his last engine early in 1826, which was Experiment built with two flues in the boiler in an effort to increase the surface heating area. Once Robert

ABOVE Four views of the various types of rail service available on the Liverpool and Manchester Railway including covered & open passenger service as well as freight & livestock shipping returned from South America the locomotive building began in earnest. In 1827 Twin Sisters was completed, a peculiar engine built especially for hauling ballast trains while building the Liverpool and Manchester Railway. As she was expected to work over some temporarily steep inclines during the construction of the railway she had been built with two boilers. This was so that which ever way the incline one boiler flue was always covered with water, and the fire in the other was allowed to die down or go out.

Robert Stephenson and Co built many further engines for collieries and the new railways that had begun to spring up around the country, and in

each of these engines there was some improvement, some refinement of the design as was seen with the Lancashire Witch built for the Bolton and Leigh Railway and then later on with Rocket. Winning the Rainhill trials was an obvious boost, as was the order for the further seven locomotives for the Liverpool and Manchester Railway.

However, the company did not rest on its laurels and continued to experiment and improve the design of each subsequent locomotive built. Thus the later engines of the "Rocket" class were built with less steeply inclined cylinders to improve their stability and the last of these, Northumbria, was the first engine to be built with a smokebox. When the Liverpool and Manchester Railway opened on 15th September 1830, the unfortunate William Huskisson, MP for Liverpool, was accidentally knocked down by Rocket during the festivities. George Stephenson driving Northumbria raced the injured man to Eccles for medical attention. He covered the fifteen miles from Parkside, the scene of the accident, to Eccles in less than twenty-five minutes, an average speed of thirty-six miles an hour. No man had ever travelled so fast before. Unfortunately, however, the mercy dash was in vain, Huskisson's injuries were too severe and he died later that night.

Eighteen months after Rainhill Rocket was extensively modified. Her chimney was shortened and remounted on the boiler on a smokebox and the incline of her cylinders was reduced so they were nearly horizontal. Despite these refinements the pace of technology was such that by 1830 Rocket and her sisters were obsolete. She still continued to work the Liverpool and Manchester until 1836 when she was sold to a colliery in Carlisle where she worked for a further three years. By then the engine was considered to be of insufficient power and too worn out to be of any further use, though fortunately she was not scrapped. In 1862 the colliery company presented the derelict remains to the Patent Office Museum, later the

OPPOSITE Robert Fairlie's double engine locomotive used on the Mexican Railway

Science Museum, where she can still be seen today.

The next significant advance in the development of the steam locomotive was Planet, completed in October 1830 for the Liverpool and Manchester Railway. This four wheeled engine had her two cylinders placed inside the frame under the smokebox where the warmth prevented the cylinders cooling and condensing the steam, an idea suggested to Stephenson by Trevithick some years before as a means of improving fuel economy. The rear wheels were driven via connecting rods to the double cranked rear axle. Two months later Mercury was completed, a sister engine in most respects except that the frames were raised above the level of the driving axle, and for freight working further similar locomotives were built with the wheels coupled together. Such was the success of these engines that their fame spread far and wide and everybody wanted one. Robert Stephenson and Co were soon swamped with orders, not only from developing railways in Britain but also those from many countries abroad who were all eager to take advantage of this new and revolutionary form of transport. Even so, there were still further improvements that could be made, as the "Planets" had proved to be unstable at speed, and their firebox capacity inadequate. Stephenson extended the locomotive frames behind the firebox and added a trailing axle to improve the stability of the engine and enable a bigger firebox to be used. Thus the "Patentee" class of locomotive was created, and many of these engines were built. They were generally of the 2-2-2 wheel arrangement with two large driving wheels on the centre axle and outside frames. It was a versatile type, able to be optimised for either passenger or freight use, and many variations were built and exported for the countless

**OPPOSITE** William Huskisson has gone down in history as being the first person to be killed in a rail accident

**BELOW** Stephenson's 'long boiler' locomotives always suffered from pitching problems

fledgling railways under construction both in Britain and around the world.

Despite the success of the "Patentee" class, Robert Stephenson knew there was still room for further improvement. In 1842 he discovered that the chimneys and smokeboxes were beginning to burn out prematurely on many of his engines and, after some experimentation, discovered that the smokeboxes were reaching a temperature in excess of 700 degrees Fahrenheit. This was, of course, a terrible waste. No useful work was performed by a red hot smokebox. Stephenson's solution to

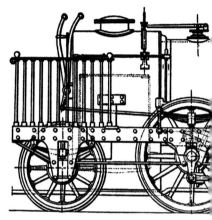

this was his 'long boilered' locomotives, where the tubes and the boiler were lengthened by between four and five feet. He also gave the new engines a large square firebox with a dome on top to collect steam for the outside cylinders. However, the three axles with the large centre driving wheel had to be crammed together under the boiler otherwise the engine would be unable to negotiate any but the most broadly radiused curves. This left the

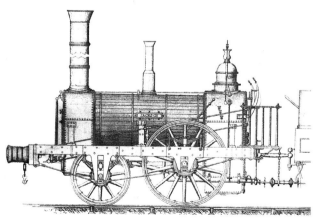

large firebox overhanging at one end and the smokebox and cylinders at the other, causing the locomotive to pitch back and forth if it began to travel at any speed. Despite a number of attempts to cure this problem by changing the wheel arrangement to 4-2-0 or even 4-2-2 with the addition of a trailing axle, the pitching motion was never completely eliminated. Because of this the 'long boiler' locomotive enjoyed limited success as a passenger hauling engine. However, as six coupled 0-6-0 engines the class were found to be very suitable for heavy goods traffic and many saw long service hauling coal trains on lines like the Stockton and Darlington where freight was the mainstay of operation.

Another important advance to come out of the workshops of Robert Stephenson and Co was what became known as 'Stephenson's link motion', though it was in fact developed by one of the company's fitters, William Howe, in 1842. This eliminated the reliability problems of the previously used fork or gab gear, and provided the engine driver with a means of "cutting off" steam for expansive working.

George Stephenson died in 1848. The company he set up in 1823 with his son had made Robert Stephenson a millionaire by the time of his death in 1859. Robert Stephenson and Co carried on building locomotives for almost another century, merging with Hawthorn Leslie and Co in 1937. More importantly, the true legacy the Stephensons left behind was the foundation of a transport system that changed the lives of millions of people all over the world forever.

**CENTRE** Stephenson experimented with various configurations of the Patentee class, including this 0-4-2 version of 1833

**OPPOSITE** Planet's cylinders were under the smokebox to keep them warm

# Chapter 5

# Alternative Practices and Other Influences

ALTHOUGH PIONEERS, THE Stephensons were far from being the only people building steam engines in those early years. Edward Bury of Liverpool, although unable to produce an engine in time for the trials at Rainhill, was an engineer of considerable skill. The engines he built were all four wheeled, either 2-2-0 or 0-4-0, and were distinctive in appearance with their inside bar frames and round dome-topped fireboxes usually finished in polished copper. Bury's engines were generally well designed and well built, and in the early years they were quite able to manage the traffic of the time. However, they were small and light in weight, and as the trains they hauled became heavier they were less able to cope satisfactorily with the loads required of them. Edward Bury was locomotive superintendent of the London and Birmingham Railway and he succeeded in persuading the board that his own small locomotives were adequate and that to build larger ones would be an unnecessary expense. The consequence of this policy was that London and Birmingham trains would frequently be double headed and sometimes three or even four locomo-

tives would be required to haul the train. Not a terribly efficient way to run a railway! However, Bury's engines had some important innovations, and the cheap, lightweight bar frames and domed topped firebox found much favour with railway lines abroad, particularly in America.

In August 1835 a new railway company was incorporated to build a line connecting Bristol to London, and to build it the board selected a brilliant young engineer named Isambard Kingdom Brunel. In 1829 Brunel had impressed many of the board members with his design of a suspension bridge that won a competition to bridge the River Avon at Bristol, and he seemed a perfect choice to build their Great Western Railway despite his comparatively young age of 29. Brunel believed in speed, he thought that the travelling public would better appreciate a journey made as in as much comfort as possible and which was as short as possible. He immediately dismissed the four foot

ABOVE Edward Bury produced small, light engines such as this 2-2-0

OPPOSITE Isambard Kingdom Brunel was chosen to build a railway from Bristol to London

eight and a half inch gauge used by
George Stephenson as being too narrow. He wanted to have engines with the
widest firebox possible in order to produce the greatest amount of steam, and
on the wider gauge coaches could be
built with a low centre of gravity and
with increased space and comfort inside
for the passengers. He decided on a
gauge of seven feet and a quarter inch
and engineered the line to be as straight
as possible, ensuring that all curves were
of the greatest possible radius. The first
engines brought in to work the line were
unsuccessful, and in 1837 he hired

another young engineer named Daniel
Gooch, then only 21, to acquire something more suitable. By a stroke of luck
a couple of large "Patentee" type locomotives originally built for the five foot
six inch gauge New Orleans Railway in
America by Robert Stephenson and Co
had been returned unsold. They were
modified for the seven foot and a quarter inch Great Western Railway and as
North Star and Morning Star turned in
some pretty impressive performances.
The first section of the line from
London to Maidenhead opened in 1838,
and in that year North Star hauled a

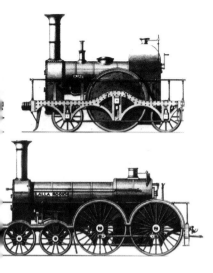

passenger train at an average speed of thirty-eight miles an hour while reaching a top speed of forty-five miles per hour. At the time this was sensational. All Brunel's theories and advocacy of the broad gauge had been vindicated. By 1841 the line to Bristol had been completed and the Great Western Railway gradually began to extend its broad gauge northwards. An intense rivalry began between the broad gauge advocates and the supporters of Stephenson's standard gauge, claims and counter claims abounded. But it was the passenger who had to put up with the chaos at break of gauge stations. Eventually the government realised that it had to act, and in 1845 a Royal Commission was set up to investigate the problem. By this time Gooch was building Great Western engines in the GWR's own workshops at Swindon. In 1846 he built a large "Patentee" type of locomotive that made a run from London to Swindon at an average speed of over 59 miles per hour. A year later by enlarging the "Patentee" design still further and adding another leading axle he created the first of the "Iron Duke" class, a 4-2-2 broad gauge engine that in its time was unrivalled for its speed and power. However, it was all to no avail, the findings of the Royal Commission clearly stated that for the railways to be of full benefit to the travelling public and to the nation in general, the gauge must be of a standard width throughout the country. And, as at that time there was 1900 miles of four foot eight and a half inch track laid against only 274 miles of

BELOW Daniel Gooch worked for Brunel as an engineer

broad gauge, standard meant standard. In May 1892 the very last broad gauge train pulled out of Paddington Station, the GWR's London terminus, with suitable crowds lining the platforms to see her off. It must have been like saying goodbye to Concorde.

The success of the large fireboxed engines on Brunel's broad gauge prompted a number of experiments with standard gauge engines in order to achieve a similar effect. One of these was Stephenson's 'long boilered' engine with a wide firebox built behind the rear axle, another was a locomotive designed by Thomas Crampton, an engineer who had spent

some time with Daniel Gooch on the Great Western. His idea was to have a deep firebox between the second and third axles with the large driving wheels mounted on the third axles, behind the firebox, giving the engine a 4-2-0 wheel arrangement. To avoid overly long connecting rods, the cylinders were brought back from the front of the engine and mounted between the first and second axles on the outside of the frames. This gave the engine the advantage of a large firebox but with good stability and none of the pitching motion experienced by 'long boilered' locomotives at high speed. In 1845 a Crampton locomotive reached a top speed of sixty-five miles per hour while hauling twelve coaches from London to Wolverton on the London and North Western Railway. Despite this success, other designs superseded the Crampton in Britain although many were built on the Continent, particularly in France and in Germany.

Yet another variation of the "Patentee" type of locomotive was designed by David Joy in 1847 for the London, Brighton and South Coast Railway. Built by E B Wilson and Co Jenny Lind had the usual "Patentee"

style double frames but had her leading and trailing axles supported by the outside frame and the driving axle supported by the inside frame. With a boiler pressure of 120lb psi, the highest known at the time, Jenny Lind ran at speeds in excess of fifty miles per hour during her first trials. She also proved to be remarkably stable due to the sideways play allowed to the leading pair of wheels by her construction. Such was the success of the locomotive that many more "Jenny Lind"s were built over a period of nearly forty years.

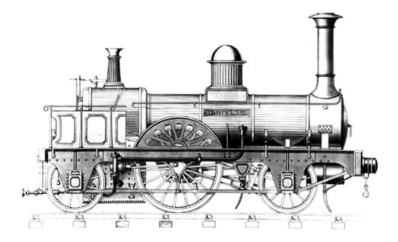

LEFT Jenny Lind had the highest boiler pressure of her time, when new in 1847

# Chapter 6

# Steam Abroad

RAILWAY MANIA WAS NOT CONFINED to the British Isles. With vast tracts of untamed country and enormous distances between major cities, America was quick to spot the advantages of the new form of transport. After some experimentation, the first commercial steam railway, the South Carolina Railroad, ran its first train on Christmas Day 1830. A train with over forty passengers on board was hauled by the brand new Best Friend of Charleston at speeds of up to twenty miles an hour. A few weeks later on 15th January 1831 the first regular train service was inaugurated and ran successfully for some months until June 1831 when Charleston's Best Friend suffered a boiler explosion.

In those early days many of the new railways that sprang up across America, purchased locomotives from Great Britain, very often from Robert Stephenson and Co. One of the better known of these imported engines was John Bull, a four wheeled "Planet" class engine that was sent in pieces to the Camden and Amboy Railroad in Pennsylvania in 1831. It was assembled by Isaac Dripps with a few modifications of his own, most notably a circular domed firebox and the very first 'pilot', a two wheeled leading bogie that assisted the locomotive in negotiating the tight curves of the lightly laid track. The 'pilot' also had a wedge shaped framework attached to the front of it designed to clear obstructions from the track before they derailed the locomotive. This device became known as a 'cowcatcher'. While standard gauge track was the most widely used throughout America (there were exceptions), the actual method of laying it was vastly different to the solid, pre-

Generally, British engines were found to be unsuitable for the rough terrain of the New World, and the American locomotive industry rapidly became a home grown affair. Bury style bar frames were almost universally adopted as they were simple to build and suitably economic. For ease of maintenance all the moving parts and fittings were placed outside the frames where possible including the cylinders and connecting rods. Two pairs of coupled

cisely engineered permanent way as seen in the UK. With enormous distances to cover over rugged and often inhospitable country American engineers had to keep the costs down if they were to have a railway at all. Instead of bullhead rail being laid in chairs, flat bottomed rails were spiked directly to the sleepers. Instead of the superbly engineered lines with tunnels, viaducts and embankments designed to keep the track as level and straight as possible, in America the track was laid over whatever was deemed the most suitable route. Sharp curves and steep inclines could often not be avoided and the locomotives used had to be capable of negotiating these hazards. And, of course, most of the land was unfenced. Dripps' 'pilot' was soon seen to be a very useful idea and with a few modifications it rapidly became standard practice on all American railroads.

**CENTRE** Early American railway pioneers worked on similar principles to their UK counterparts

**BELOW** John Bull, built by Robert Stephenson in 1831 for the Camden and Amboy Railroad of New Jersey, USA

RIGHT Grass Hopper was an unusual 0-4-0 US locomotive

driving wheels were favoured as the resulting short wheel base enabled the locomotive to negotiate tight curves especially with the four wheel front bogie to guide it. A bell and a loud whistle were fitted to the engine in order to warn all creatures, four or two legged, of the locomotive's impending approach, and the cow-catcher took care of any that were too slow, too deaf or too stubborn. A powerful lamp was fitted to the front of the engine to provide further warning after dark. The locomotives were built with comfortable and roomy cabs to protect the crew from the bitter winters and, as they were mostly fired with wood, they were fitted with large conical 'spark arresting' chim-

neys. This distillation of ideas became the standard American 4-4-0. Versatile, ubiquitous, many hundreds were built travelling many thousands of miles as they criss crossed America, connecting the populations of each coast with the settlements of the interior. Variations of this type were in use for decades from the mid to late nineteenth century. Although the distances covered were vast the travelling speeds of the American trains were slow compared to the speed of trains in Britain and Europe. Frequent stops were required to refuel and water both the locomotive and the passengers, and long journeys must have been fairly tedious affairs. However, to anyone faced with a similar journey

in a stagecoach, a steam train would have been an utter godsend, a true miracle of technology.

Initially, railways in Europe tended to be built much like those in Britain. Standard gauge with rails set in chairs was the most usual type of track laid, and many of the first locomotives used on these lines were imported from Britain, often from Robert Stephenson and Co

Typical of these was the first steam engine to run in Germany, Adler, a small "Patentee" type that was exported from England, complete with an English driver, for the Nuremburg-Fürth Railway which opened in 1835. Robert Stephenson and Co also licensed construction companies in other countries to build engines to their designs. The first engine to run in Belgium was a "Patentee" built locally

ABOVE US engines soon developed their own style, with cowcatchers, large front lamps and wide spark-arresting chimney. This is a Baldwin 2-6-0 built in 1883

**RIGHT** Adler was the first steam engine to run in Germany, in 1835, and was an English Patentee type machine

under just such an arrangement and was called Le Belge. Italy's first engine was a "Patentee", as was the first engine to run on Russian metals on the St Petersburg to Pavlovsk railway opened in 1838. Another "Patentee" for Germany was built under license in Munich in 1841 by Joseph von Maffei, founder of a company that would become one of the leading locomotive manufacturers in Europe. Holland's first steam engines were two "Patentees" named Arend and Snelheid which worked the line from Amsterdam to Haarlem opened in 1839. A "Patentee" was the first locomotive to run on the inaugural five miles of track between Naples and Portici in the Kingdom of Naples. This engine was also built under license but by another Newcastle company, probably Robert Stephenson and Co could not keep up with the demand.

France had her own pioneer, Marc Séguin, who in 1829, wholly independently of the Stephensons' work with

Rocket, built a steam locomotive with a multi-tubular boiler to run on the line from St Etienne to Andrézieux. However, instead of using exhaust from the cylinders to draw the fire via a blast pipe in the chimney, he developed a complicated system of draughting using two large fans mounted on the tender and driven by belts from the trailing axle. The mechanics of this system proved to be unreliable and the engine was not a success as there was never sufficient draught on the fire. In France at this time the railways were generally regarded as little more than a mechanical oddity, and it was not until 1837 when the Péreire brothers opened the short line from Paris to St Germain that the French public began to realise what the rest of the world was on about. In 1842 the French government passed its Railway Law and from that time all railways were planned and built under strict government control. Among early locomotives used were

the ubiquitous "Patentee" type, sometimes heavily modified. Later the Crampton style locomotive with single driving wheels mounted on the trailing axle proved popular, and many variations of these were seen on the lines running into and out of Paris.

As the years progressed, with experience and experimentation, most countries gradually developed their own locomotives and the means to construct them according to local conditions and requirements. However, the basic formula for every successful locomotive built can be traced back to Rocket, and the ingenuity of the Stephensons.

BELOW The French were slow to adopt railways, but soon began building their own destinctive engines

# Chapter 7

# Further Developments

AS THE DESIGN OF THE STEAM locomotive improved and the railway system was extended throughout the country, more people began to travel further and faster than even before. With the introduction of dining cars and sleeping cars trains rapidly became heavier and heavier. To cope with these increasing loads bigger engines were built with ever larger fireboxes and boilers. The 2-2-2 locomotive with the single pair of driving wheels was still in general use for passenger work during the latter part of the nineteenth century, the design being enlarged and improved according to the requirements of the operating company. Many of the smaller lines slowly amalgamated to pool their resources and consolidate their respective shares of the market. In 1846 the Liverpool and Manchester joined with the London and Birmingham, the Manchester and Birmingham and the Grand Junction Railway to form the London and North Western Railway. The responsibilities for producing locomotive power for the LNWR was initially split between the Southern Division, based at Wolverton, and the Northern Division, based at Crewe. Each division had its own works and locomotive superintendent, and their philosophy and practice differed enormously. In charge of the Wolverton works was J E McConnell who had previously been the superintendent of the Birmingham and Gloucester Railway based at Bromsgrove. In the year prior to the LNWR amalgamation he had designed and built a number of engines with inside frames and inside bearings, and these had been a great success. The first engines he built at Wolverton were an enlarged version of the BGR locomotives with large boilers and six foot six inch driving wheels. The high open splashers and the lack of an outside bearing to the driving wheels gave the engines a 'leggy' appearance, rapidly earning them the nickname 'Bloomers' after one Mrs Bloomer, a lady from America who was then championing the simplification of women's dress, including, horror of horrors, the wearing of trousers. Later versions of these engines had seven foot driving wheels, and in 1852 he designed a still larger locomotive with seven foot six driving wheels. At this time it was generally believed that engines should be built

BELOW The West Coast Express being hauled by a Bloomer locomotive in 1865

with the boiler positioned as low as possible within the frames to give as low a centre of gravity as possible and thus, so it was thought, better stability. The only problem with this philosophy was that the diameter of the driving wheels was necessarily restricted. McConnell disagreed with this theory; he believed that a high boilered engine was just as stable as long as it was properly constructed. The 'Bloomers' proved him right.

In complete contrast to the practice at Wolverton, the locomotive superintendent of the Northern Division of the LNWR at Crewe, Alexander Allan, favoured small locomotives. Some years before, The Grand Junction Railway had had several "Patentee" locomotives which had suffered broken crank axles. Allan had overcome this problem by rebuilding the engines with outside cylinders, creating what became known as the 'Crewe' type of locomotive. In common with Edward Bury, Allan believed that small engines were cheaper to build and to operate than large engines - which was true up to a point. As train loads became heavier more power was required to haul them, and for the Northern Division of the LNWR this meant that it was necessary

to couple two, three, or sometimes even four engines together to haul one train. Any savings made by building small locomotives were more than expended in the cost of the manpower required to drive and service them. Nonetheless, the 'Crewe' type of engine proved to be successful and reliable and nearly four hun-

CENTRE Francis Trevithick designed this 2-2-2 Single with its large driving wheels in 1845

dred of them were built between 1845 and 1858, about a third of these being 2-2-2 types for passenger trains and the rest built as 2-4-0s for hauling freight. The livery of the Northern Division was a dark green colour, and passengers who had travelled up from London behind the large bright red Southern Division

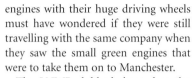

engines with their huge driving wheels must have wondered if they were still travelling with the same company when they saw the small green engines that were to take them on to Manchester.

The LNWR dubbed themselves the 'Premier Line' and in their publicity campaigns their London terminus at Euston was much touted as being the 'Gateway to the North'. It was therefore a source of great annoyance to the LNWR directors that the publicity machine of the Great Western Railway was claiming faster and faster speeds for their express trains, especially as the famed broad gauge lines were gradually creeping ever northwards. They commissioned the Crewe works of the Northern Division to build three experimental express locomotives with the idea of proving to themselves and to the travelling public that standard gauge engines were just as good as anything running on the broad

gauge. The three locomotives were completed in 1847. One was Courier, a Crampton with seven foot driving wheels mounted behind the firebox, another was Velocipede, designed by Alexander Allan, who thought that the very idea of the 'contest' was absurd and so did no more than build an enlarged version of his usual design with seven foot driving wheels. The third engine was designed by the Locomotive Superintendent of the Northern Division, Francis Trevithick (son of Richard), who conversely to Allan thought it was vitally important not only to equal but to surpass the performance of the Great Western engines. Accordingly he designed a locomotive with eight foot six inch driving wheels, the largest to run on standard gauge track. As it was still considered desirable for an engine to have a low centre of gravity at the time, the boiler was placed underneath the driving axle with outside cylinders providing the motive force. The locomotive was named Cornwall, and she proved to be a success from her very first trial run as she reached the speed of seventy nine miles per hour, one mile an hour faster than the speeds claimed by the Great Western engine. Cornwall was exhibited at the Great Exhibition of 1851 where she attracted a great deal of interest. In later years she was rebuilt by John Ramsbottom with the boiler placed above the driving axle, and in this condition she gave many years of useful service hauling express trains between Liverpool and Manchester. Towards the end of the nineteenth century some fifty years later Cornwall was still considered to be one of the fastest engines in service provided she was not overloaded. One of the first locomotives to be deliberately earmarked for preservation, Cornwall can be seen today in the collection of the National Railway Museum at York.

In 1857 John Ramsbottom succeeded Trevithick as Chief Mechanical Engineer of the Northern Division of the London and North Western Railway. His first express engine was a 2-2-2 'single' with driving wheels of seven feet seven and a half inches and the unprepossessing name Problem. Two important innovations helped to make the class one of the outstanding performers of its time. They were the first engines to be fitted with steam driven injectors to refill the boiler instead of the feed water pump that had been the only device previously available. The injector was the invention of a Frenchman named Henri Giffard, at the time more well known for his steam driven hydrogen(!) filled airships. The other advance

**LEFT** John Ramsbottom, Chief Mechanical Engineer of the Northern Division of the LNWR

was truly home grown, invented by Ramsbottom himself; the water trough. "Problem" class engines were all fitted with the scoops necessary to take water at high speed and consequently were the first locomotives capable of sustained high speed running. One of the class with the more romantic name Lady of the Lake was awarded a bronze medal at the Exhibition of 1862. In all, sixty of these locomotives were built and as a class they proved themselves to be fast, reliable and remarkably long lived in service. When in late 1861 McConnell resigned from the Southern Division, the premises at Wolverton became the London and North Western Railway's carriage works and Ramsbottom was appointed Locomotive Superintendent at Crewe, responsible for all of the LNWR's motive power. Ramsbottom largely left McConnell's 'Bloomers' alone as they were still capable of keeping time with the London to Birmingham expresses. However, most of the Allan or Trevithick locomotives of the Northern Division, with the exception of Cornwall which was rebuilt, were soon scrapped in favour of his own "Problem" class engines. For freight work Ramsbottom built an

0-6-0 tender known as the "DX Goods" of which no less than 943 were built between 1855 and 1872. These engines were simple yet strong and robust and, with a few modifications, the class had a long service life with some examples still working up until 1930.

The Great Northern Railway was incorporated in 1846 to build a line from London to York via Grantham, Retford and Doncaster, and by 1852 this was completed all the way to their London terminus at King's Cross. Engines to work the line were built by R & W Hawthorn and Co. of Newcastle, an experienced firm who had built engines for Timothy Hackworth of the Stockton and Darlington. For the Great Northern they built twenty 2-2-2 locomotives which were updated versions of the "Patentee". Later they built a further batch of similar but much larger

OPPOSITE A LNWR Problem class engine on the West Coast Postal run

BELOW A DX Goods speeds over Bushy water troughs on an 'up' goods train for London. Water troughs were invented by John Ramsbottom

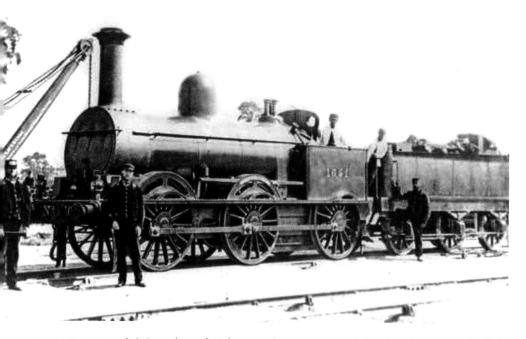

ABOVE A DX Goods 0-6-0 in early guise on the LNWR

2-2-2 engines that became known, inevitably, as "Large Hawthorns". Built with six foot six inch driving wheels and large boilers, these engines were excellent express passenger locomotives of their day, and were entrusted with the London to York section of the new Flying Scotsman passenger service out of King's Cross. At Retford the line was crossed by the Manchester, Sheffield and Lincolnshire Railway and on one occasion a signalling error allowed a MSLR freight train to lumber its way over the crossing, directly in the path of a "Large Hawthorn" at the head of an express bound for York. The Great Northern driver, realising that he had no hope of stopping his train, threw open the regulator and ploughed into the freight train at full speed. The lightly built timber wagons shattered to matchwood but the "Large Hawthorn" kept her feet and the express carried on safely northward.

The Flying Scotsman service was created to provide an express link from London to Edinburgh via the Great Northern Railway from London to York, the North Eastern Railway from York to Berwick and the North British Railway from Berwick to Edinburgh. An obvious requirement was to make the journey time as short as possible and to this end the GNR locomotive superintendent, Archibald Sturrock, designed a still larger locomotive in the hope of reducing the travelling time to eight hours. Built by R & W Hawthorn in 1853, this

BELOW The first of the Stirling Singles No 1, which is now kept at York

## FURTHER DEVELOPMENTS

engine had two pairs of leading wheels and single driving wheels seven feet in diameter. Unfortunately it was too large and too heavy and due to the rigid wheelbase of the leading axles showed some tendency for derailment. The wheels were later removed and replaced in a bogie which considerably improved the engine and she worked until 1870 though no more were built.

One of the most celebrated locomotive designs ever must surely be the eight foot diameter single drivers built by new Great Northern Locomotive Superintendent Patrick Sterling in 1870. Rightly described as a 'work of art' they were a most handsome, efficient, reliable and very fast express passenger locomotive. Of the 4-2-2 wheel arrangement, they had a leading four wheel bogie with a long wheelbase, outside cylinders and a large firebox supported by the trailing wheels. The large domeless boiler with the elegant brass safety valve cover was one of the most visually striking features of these engines which saw great service on the London to York section of the Flying Scotsman express. On a number of occasions the 'Stirling Singles' were timed at speeds of up to seventy five miles per hour. Fifty three of the class

were built and they were the mainstay of the GNR's express traffic until the closing years of the nineteenth century when the increasing weight of the trains demanded still larger engines. The 'Stirling Singles' were all withdrawn by 1916 though the first, No. 1, has been preserved at the National Railway Museum at York.

The Midland Railway was formed in 1844 from a number of smaller railways including the Midland Counties Railway, the North Midland Railway and the Birmingham and Derby Junction Railway. From 1853 many railways were experimenting with various means by which they could burn coal instead of coke including complicated firebox designs, boilers with combustion chambers and weird and wonderful grates.

The Midland Railway instead came up with the idea of having a brick arch placed in the firebox, a baffle plate at the top of the firehole and a fire door which could be used to control the flow of cold air into the firebox. These devices used in conjunction with a steam operated 'blower' that directed a stream of air through the firebox and up the chimney proved to be all that was required to ensure that a coal fired locomotive would 'consume its own smoke'. The Locomotive Superintendent, Matthew Kirtley, was also one of the first to design an express passenger locomotive with more than one pair of driving wheels. In 1870, as a development of the previous similar though smaller engines, he designed the '800 class'. These were 2-4-0s with outside frames, inside cylinders and two pairs of coupled driving wheels six feet eight inches in diameter. Free steaming and steady riding the '800 class' locomotives were a firm favourite with their crews, and they proved to be fast and reliable operators of the Midland's Anglo-Scottish express traffic. A year later Kirtley introduced a similar engine with a larger boiler and with the driving axle bearings inside the frames. These were the '890 class', some of which were especially modified with a centre buffer at the rear of the tender to enable them to haul the new American Pullman cars first imported by the Midland Railway. The forty-eight members of the '800 class' had long working lives, the last being scrapped in 1936 after more than sixty years service.

# Chapter 8

# Competition in the South

AS WE HAVE ALREADY SEEN THERE was considerable competition between the various railway companies for the prestige, and the ticket revenue, of having the best and fastest express between London and the Scottish cities. Such rivalry also existed between the southern railway companies who competed for traffic from London to the various ports on the south coast. Heavier, more comfortable trains with dining cars and sleeping cars required larger and more powerful locomotives. The single driver was still the most usual arrangement for express passenger engines, with larger boilers, higher working pressures and increased cylinder size giving each successive design progressively more power and speed.

The London and South Western Railway was first incorporated in 1839 and opened lines to Southampton and Portsmouth in 1840 and 1842 respectively. It was not long before the LSWR began to look further afield, to Salisbury, Bournemouth, Exeter, Plymouth and even the Cornish coast. This was, of course, Great Western territory, and the LSWR had to build some sprightly engines to compete with the famed broad gauge locomotives of Daniel Gooch. During his time as LSWR locomotive superintendent Joseph Beattie built a number of 2-4-0 express locomotives for the London to Salisbury and the London to

## COMPETITION IN THE SOUTH

Beattie was succeeded by his son, William Beattie, who, following some unsuccessful experiments with piston valves (he was a little ahead of his time), was replaced by William Adams in 1878. Adams was an experienced locomotive engineer having previously been locomotive superintendent for the North London and the Great Eastern Railways before joining the LSWR, and he soon began to produce express engines able to maintain the scheduled services from London.

LEFT A Beattie 2-4-0 being used to pull a china clay train

Bournemouth services. Introduced between 1859 and 1860 these engines gave good service despite suffering somewhat from their creator's passion for gadgets. The fireboxes were complicated affairs with 'mid-feathers', an early form of thermic syphon, and different combustion chambers designed to get the maximum amount of steam out of every last ounce of coal. For even greater thermal efficiency, Beattie had devised a way of heating the boiler feed water with exhaust steam from the cylinders. Unfortunately the boilers proved to be prone to leakage and the saving in coal was outweighed by the cost of the extra maintenance required to keep the engines running. Joseph

There was another railway company competing for the lucrative traffic to Portsmouth and that was the London, Brighton and South Coast Railway. Incorporated in 1846 as a result of the combination of the London and Brighton and the London and Croydon Railways, the LBSC spread its tentacles as far as Portsmouth in the west and Hastings in the east. While their lines to Brighton and the important port at Newhaven enjoyed a complete monopoly the railway was often engaged in sometimes fierce rivalry with both the London and South Western and the London, Chatham and Dover Railway to the east. The LBSC ensured their public image was kept up to scratch by

ABOVE LBSC locomotives were finished in 'improved engine green'

successive generations of superb locomotives renowned not only for their innovation of design and fine performances but also for their generally striking appearance. After Joy's "Jenny Lind"s, the most celebrated creations of the succeeding locomotive superintendent, John Craven, were his 2-2-2 engines with six foot six inch single driving wheels built in 1862. Later engines of the LBSC were particularly noted for their outstanding livery of "improved engine green", actu-

ally a shade of yellow ochre, introduced by William Stroudley, locomotive superintendent from 1870 to 1889. The colourful paintwork was far from Stroudley's only contribution, he was also one of the first locomotive engineers to give some thought to the standardisation of parts and fittings that could be made common to the various classes of engines in his charge. His first designs included the "Terrier"s, small but useful and long lived 0-6-0 tank engines, and a

2-2-2 express engine with six foot nine inch driving wheels named Grosvenor. On one of its trials this engine hauled a train of twenty-two coaches from Brighton to London without any loss of time. A further development of the 2-2-2 type led to the twenty-four strong "G" class with six foot six inch driving wheels introduced in 1881 for the London to Portsmouth expresses. These engines turned in quite remarkable performances over the sometimes steeply graded line across the North Downs, a duty they continued to fulfil until the early years of the twentieth century. With train loads gradually getting heavier Stroudley had to build a more powerful locomotive for the important London to Brighton expresses. His success with the "G" class led him to try a 0-4-2 wheel arrangement with two pairs of driving wheels the same size as those of the "G", namely six foot six inches. The first of these engines, Gladstone, was completed in 1882 and attracted some criticism for the unusual wheel arrangement. However, in service Gladstone proved to be fast and extremely powerful for her size and, in spite of the concerns over the leading coupled driving wheels, she was smooth running and rode well at speed. A further thirty five "Gladstone"s were built, one of which, Edward Blount, was shown at the Paris Exhibition in 1889 and won a gold medal. The "Gladstone"s in their striking ochre livery became the best known of all Stroudley's locomotives. They had a long working life, the last one was not withdrawn until 1932, and the first of

BELOW An 0-6-0 Terrier in rare unrebuilt form

the class is preserved at the National Railway Museum at York.

It seems that some of the success of the "Gladstone"'s' design rubbed off onto the rival LSWR camp at Nine Elms. William Adams produced a similar 0-4-2 design from the company workshops in 1887, Queen Victoria's Jubilee year, the class being subsequently known as the "Jubilees". Intended for mixed traffic duties they had slightly smaller driving wheels than the "Gladstone"'s, six foot rather than six foot six inches, but had the same size cylinders with the steam chests built underneath. With their Adams style stove pipe chimneys and the LSWR's pale green livery they looked quite different, and, like the "Gladstone"'s, they were reliable performers and gave many years service. Indeed the last members of the ninety strong class were still working after World War II and were not scrapped until 1948.

Notwithstanding the success of the "Jubilees", William Adams is probably best remembered for the beautiful 4-4-0 express engines he built for the London and South Western Railway. Sixty of these engines were built between 1891 and 1896, some with six foot seven inch driving wheels and the others with seven foot one inch driving wheels, and they all had outside cylinders with inside slide valves worked by Stephenson's link motion. The engines were built for the London to Bournemouth and London to Exeter expresses, and on these duties they were often timed at speeds of up to eighty miles per hour. The locomotives were fitted with Adams' own design of four wheel leading bogie which he had first patented in 1863, and which gave the 4-4-0s superior riding qualities and great stability at speed. Although these engines began to be withdrawn in 1930 a small number contin-

ued in service throughout World War II, and the last one, No 563, was fortuitously restored for the centennial exhibition at Waterloo station in 1948. This engine is now in the National collection.

BELOW Dugald Drummond's T9 4-4-0s were introduced in 1899 on the L&SWR and they have often been described as his most successful

# Chapter 9

# Railway Rivalry

COMPETITION FOR TRAFFIC BET-ween railway companies was often fierce, especially where main line routes were duplicated. The situation was exacerbated where one railway could only reach its destination by means of 'running powers' over a competitor's existing line. Such circumstances could be the cause of anything from the outbreak of fisticuffs that frequently occurred at Havant Station in 1859 when the first LSWR trains tried to reach Portsmouth over LBSC rails, to the building of an entire new line. The Midland Railway, fed up with the delays on the stretch of LNWR metals they had been forced to use to get to Carlisle, built their own line from Settle, creating one of the most celebrated and breathtakingly scenic railways in Britain in the process. The routes north

from London to Aberdeen, Glasgow and Edinburgh were particularly fiercely contested. With the LNWR running on the west coast route and the GNR/NER on the east coast, both companies used their considerable publicity machines to promote their respective superiority. Central to the claims and counter claims was, of course, the creation of the motive power necessary to haul the ever heavier trains at faster and faster speeds to their destination. On the LNWR Ramsbottom's "Problem"s of 1859 were still in service and two of them, Waverley and Marmion gave a good account of themselves during the railway "races" of 1888 when they ran non stop on the London to Crewe section of the 10.00am express service to Edinburgh. They were competing with the Great Northern's 10.00am Flying Scotsman service from Kings Cross to York hauled by the fast and powerful eight foot singles of Patrick Stirling. Further north the challenge was taken up on the east coast by the North Eastern Railway from York to Berwick and by the North British Railway from Berwick to Edinburgh. On the west coast route the LNWR carried on from Crewe to Carlisle, and from there the Caledonian Railway continued on to Edinburgh. The gradual and successive reduction of journey times over each route attracted much public interest, and many of the engineering journals of the day published the train timings achieved by each of the railway companies involved. The west coast route was at a slight disadvantage, however, being both slightly longer and rather steeper in places than the east coast route. Eventually the GNR/NER companies managed to pare the journey down

ABOVE The Forth Bridge opened in 1890, reducing the distance from Edinburgh to Aberdeen by 30 miles

OPPOSITE The Settle to Carlisle line passes through the most breathtaking countryside, including the famous Ribblehead Viaduct

ABOVE Hardwicke, a 2-4-0 Precedent, averaged 67mph from Crewe to Carlisle in 1895

to seven hours twenty-seven minutes inclusive of a twenty-five minute meal break at York, although it is doubtful that the passengers would have thought this minor miracle to be of any great benefit as they bumped along at breakneck speeds in rigid six wheeled coaches. The LNWR just could not compete with this, and in the end common sense prevailed and the rival factions agreed on a minimum journey time of eight and a half hours. For a while.

In 1890 the North British Railway opened their celebrated bridge across the Firth of Forth reducing the distance from Edinburgh to Aberdeen by some thirty miles. Five years later the LNWR reduced the journey time of their overnight train

to Aberdeen, and the GNR/NER followed suit with a twenty minute cut in their own overnight schedules. The LNWR responded to this with a further cut of forty minutes and the "Race to Aberdeen" was on. An important element of the LNWR's success was a class of small locomotives designed by John Ramsbottom's successor, Francis Webb, and introduced in 1874. These diminutive 2-4-0s, known as the "Precedent"s, were the first engines to be built with their internal steam passages made as short and as direct as possible. This design feature ensured the "Precedent"s were extremely fast and powerful for their size, and in August 1895 one of the class, Hardwicke, covered the one hundred and forty one miles from Crewe to Carlisle at an average speed of sixty-seven miles per hour. True, the train hauled was only seventy tons in weight, but there were some fearsome gradients to overcome including, of course, Shap. On this occasion the entire five hundred and forty mile journey from Euston to Aberdeen was completed in less than nine hours including three stops to change engines, and the average speed achieved overall was sixty three and a half miles per hour. The event made international news, though the hapless passengers may well have wondered why it was necessary for them to arrive at their destination at five o'clock in the morning! After this momentous run the railway companies decided they had gone far enough and that more sensible timings should be re-introduced before there was a serious accident. No doubt this decision was a source of great relief to the passengers. One hundred and fifty-five "Precedent"s were built at Crewe works and they had long and useful lives, the last one being withdrawn in 1932. Hardwicke is preserved as part of the National collection in the railway museum at York.

The Midland Railway had a somewhat different approach to wooing the Anglo-Scottish traffic. From the Pullman Palace Car Company of America sufficient parts were imported to build eighteen Pullman carriages at the Midland's Derby works. In 1874 day and night Pullman services were introduced between St Pancras and Bradford, and when the Settle to Carlisle line was completed in 1876 the Midland was able to offer similar services to Edinburgh. The railway also scrapped their third class accommodation and re-designated their standard second class coaches as third, thus providing an unprecedented standard of comfort to even the lowest fare paying-passengers. This move did not go down well with the Midland's eastern

BELOW A Webb 4-4-0 pulling a London to Scotland express in the late 19th century

expresses, the Midland needed the extra adhesion provided by the 2-4-0s due to the many steep gradients on their lines. The "800" class were particularly well designed and were the prime haulers of the Midland Railway's crack expresses. When Samuel Johnson succeeded Kirtley as the Midland's CME in 1874 he rebuilt these engines with bigger boilers and slightly larger cylinders, though he kept the original frames and motion. He also added a small cab and the Johnson 'signature' of a gracefully tapered brass safety valve cover. In this form one of these engines, No. 815, made a notable run from Carlisle to the summit of Ais Gill, covering the forty eight and a half miles in fifty nine minutes. Not so remarkable, one might think when comparing this to the exploits of the 'racing' rivals of the east and west coasts. However, No. 815 was hauling a one hundred and thirty ton train up a total rise of eleven hundred feet, the last eleven miles being a one in one hundred gradient. Such was the Midland Railway. In their rebuilt form the forty eight members of the "800" class were very popular with engine crews as they would do anything asked of them. Most of these locomotives had long service lives of some fifty years, many of them

and western rivals who were eventually forced to follow suit.

The Midland locomotives built to haul the Scottish expresses have already been briefly discussed. They were the two classes of 2-4-0 engines built by Matthew Kirtley known simply as the "800" class and the "890" class. The latter engines were especially adapted with a central buffer to haul the complete Pullman trains on the St Pancras to Bradford services. Later, when the Pullman coaches were split up to work the Scottish services their buffers were rebuilt with two side buffers as is normal British practice, and the "890" class had their centre buffers removed. Although at this time other railways were almost exclusively using 'single' driver engines for their best passing into LMS service in 1923.

Interestingly, in 1887, after having built four coupled engines for some thirteen years, and at a time when other railways thought such things obsolete, Samuel Johnson designed a 4-2-2 'single' driver express engine with seven foot four inch driving wheels. This change of tack was brought about by the invention of steam sanding gear which gave the locomotive extra adhesion when starting off or climbing a steep gradient, and allowed Johnson to make use of the uncomplicated free running qualities of a 'single driver'. With their graceful lines enhanced by the curves of the running plate and splashers and finished in the fabulous crimson lake livery adopted by the Midland Railway in the 1880s, these engines were a work of art rivalled only by the Great Northern's Stirling singles. They were also extremely fast and could reach speeds of over ninety miles an hour and maintain average speeds in excess of sixty miles per hour. Like Kirtley's "800"s, the locomotives were popular with their crews as they were smooth riding and light on coal. The engines gained the nickname "Spinners" as sometimes they would slip a little when starting a heavy train, even when the sanding gear was used. The great driving wheels would rotate smoothly without any of the bump and clatter that would be felt and heard while a coupled engine was slipping. A Johnson "Spinner" was exhibited at the Paris Exhibition of 1889 and was awarded a gold medal.

As the twentieth century took over from the nineteenth century, so the queen who had presided over that vigorous and inventive era passed on also. While royal patronage had been a prize some railways had gone to extreme lengths to win, it was one of Adams' humble "Jubilees" of 1887 that hauled the funeral train over LSWR metals on 2nd February 1901.

BELOW Samuel Johnson's 4-2-2s were nicknamed 'Spinners' because their wheels slipped a little when starting off

# Chapter 10

# Standardisation and Imported Technology

DANIEL GOOCH OF THE GREAT Western Railway imposed a degree of discipline on the seven manufacturers that produced the "Firefly" class between 1840 and 1842. This early example of standardisation continued to be the hallmark of Great Western design from 1903 when Churchward took over from Dean and became CME.

As Dean's chief assistant, Churchward had designed the boiler for the "Atbara" 4-4-0s built in 1900. In order to improve steaming rates without causing foaming in the constricted area above the firebox he used the flat topped Belpaire style boiler. This gave a maximum of water area and steam space over the firebox crown. Steam for the cylinders was drawn

from a collector pipe within the Belpaire and not from a dome on the boiler barrel. These locos were deemed unattractive by many.

The next change was the tapering of boiler barrels so that more water was carried at the hot firebox end of the boiler and less at the colder chimney end. This was first done on the "City" class 4-4-0s of 1903. Apart from the very first 4-6-0 No 100 built before 1903, tapered boilers became the standard type to be fitted on all subsequent main line locomotives.

The tapered boiler with its enlarged space over the firebox was an import from American practice, though the Belpaire shape was a Belgian design named after its inventor. Churchward used a long thirty-inch piston stroke and supplied steam by piston valves that were more than half the diameter of the pistons. With a valve gear that gave long travel and direct steam passages there was minimum restriction on the flow of steam into and out of the cylinders at high speeds.

The principle of using steam twice, known as compounding, was being used successfully in France on the Nord Railway, so Churchward bought a four

cylindered compound design by de Glehn called La France and did some comparative trials. The Great Western locomotive was No 171, a 4-6-0 called Albion which had the high boiler pressure of 225lbs psi. La France's boiler pressure was 227lbs psi. No 171 showed up well even after it was converted to a 4-4-2 in order to make the comparison fairer. The long stroke pistons seemed to develop as much energy from the steam as was the case on the French locomotive with two stages of compounding. Compounds interpose a second set of cylinders between the first set and the chimney. The exhaust steam

OPPOSITE A Great Western engine designed by Alfred de Glehn

BELOW Sir John Aspinall's huge 4-4-2s were nicknamed 'High Flyers' due to their top-heavy appearance

ABOVE WP Reid's North British Atlantic of 1906 had a Belpaire firebox and outside axleboxes under the cab

that usually escapes into the sky via the chimney is instead diverted to push again, against larger pistons because of the lower pressure.

The Great Western engine was cheaper, being a simple, and no great improvement of savings seemed to accrue from the compounding principle. However, the French machine ran very smoothly. Its four cylinders were arranged to drive on two axles. The inside cylinders drove the leading axle, the outside cylinders drove the middle axle. This meant that the opposed big end masses could balance out the tendency of long stroke pistons to transmit up and down and back and forth forces through the axleboxes. In 1905 a further test using No 40 North Star, a newly built four cylindered "Atlantic" or 4-4-2 with divided drive as above took place. Two more de Glehn compounds of the latest improved design were bought and operated in competition with No 40. The results showed that expensive compounding did not show sufficient economy over Churchward's four cylinders simple design to warrant a change of policy. As a result the "Star" class fitted with Walschaerts (Belgian) inside valve

gear set the standard Great Western express design for the next fifty years.

Most British locomotives at this time supplied saturated steam to their cylinders. In other words, the steam was not much hotter than the water it rose out of. if the saturated "wet steam" is reheated on its way to the cylinders. In special elements or thin tubes, the result will be "dry" or superheated steam at much increased temperatures. This principle was applied after 1905 to all Great Western express locomotives.

Water that is fed into boilers from tenders or tanks was generally to the coolest end of the barrel and into the

**BELOW** McKintosh's 4-6-0 of 1906 had inside cylinders and Stephenson's valve gear

boiler water. After 1911, all Great Western boilers had the water feed clacks put above the water line, i.e. via top feed fittings, and this was a modern innovation that other railways only adopted many years later. Lastly, Swindon standardised the controls and fittings within locomotive cabs to such a high degree that GWR enginemen were instantly at home in the cabs of any Swindon built locomotive. The next real push for standardisation resulted from the appointment of Swindon-trained William Stanier as CME to the LMS.

Away from the Great Western Railway the use of parallel boilers continued to create the classic British locomotive that was elegant to the eye and not so "American". Sir John Aspinall's huge 4-4-2s on the Lancashire and Yorkshire Railway, nicknamed "High Flyers", are probably the most typical example of this straight up and down style. The nickname derived from the seven foot three driving wheels was also a good description of this generally top heavy locomotive. Trouble was experienced with hot axle boxes which were inside

**BELOW** The L&SWR Urie N15 Class was considered very modern in 1918

the frames and too near the ashpan. Around 1915 outside bearings were fitted to the offending trailing wheels.

It would be impossible in a book of this size to mention more than a fraction of the locomotive designs to be found in Britain around this date. There were more than a hundred railway companies! If we continue to compare "Atlantics" however, the North British example built by W P Reid in 1906 was also a high built locomotive. It had a Belpaire firebox and outside axleboxes under the cab. Although it had outside cylinders the valve gear was, as usual, tucked away between the frames.

The 1903 North Eastern "Atlantic"'s, Class V by William Worsdell, had round topped fireboxes and a large five foot six diameter boiler. From an engine driver's point of view the most nightmarish design must have been another North Eastern "Atlantic" designed by Sir Vincent Raven in 1911. This three cylindered locomotive had all three cylinders in line and drove the front coupled axle. There were three sets of Stephenson's valve driven off six eccentrics with a connecting rod, big end, crank and webs all jammed between the frames and under the five foot six diameter boiler. The poor wretch who had the job of oiling up this part of the engine alone would have attended to at least thirty two oiling points. All of them within a most congested tangle of machinery.

It is strange that each of these designs feature longish but narrow fireboxes. The 4-4-2 wheelbase, like the 4-6-2, allows the designer to place a wide and reasonably deep firebox over the small trailing wheels. This is, of course, what Ivatt did on the Great Northern. He introduced the

first "Atlantics" to Britain in 1898, but these had narrow fireboxes. His next and very successful design made better use of the opportunity to place a short wide firebox across the frames and trailing wheels. This large boilered class of "Atlantic"s appeared in 1902. The first eighty one were un-superheated and had balanced slide valves, but the last ten were superheated with piston valves. They were a great success being both fast and strong. No 251, the first of its class, has been preserved. In 1953 it was coupled to a preserved small "Atlantic" Henry Oakley hauling a special train to Doncaster, taking 192 minutes to do the 156 mile journey. Ted Hailstone and Bill Hoole were the drivers. On the LBSC Douglas Earle Marsh, one time chief assistant to Ivatt, built two classes of large boilered

"Atlantic"s which were almost identical to the Great Northern machines. They were known as classes "H1" and "H2". The "H2"s, built in 1911, were superheated. Marsh's "I3" "Atlantic" tanks had demonstrated the value of superheating when they outperformed LNWR tender engines running between Rugby and Brighton on the 'Sunny South Express'.

Finally, here are a couple examples of 'traditional' versus the 'new'. Compare McIntosh's Caledonian Railway "Cardean" class 4-6-0 produced in 1906, with R W Urie's "N15" class 4-6-0 built for the London and South Western Railway in 1918. The "Cardean"s had inside cylinders and Stephenson's valve gear which drove slide valves above the cylinders through rockers. The running plate was low and the coupling rod would disappear within its splashers every half turn of the wheels. David Gibson drove No 903 for five years and must have been a proud man to have charge of such an impressive machine. The LSWR "N15" class were, in contrast, a very modern concept in 1918. Not only did they expose almost the whole diameter of their driving wheels as a result of the high running plate but all the movements of the Walschaerts valve gear as well. Drivers could oil and examine the valve gear without squeezing between the frames. The "N15"s which had short travel valves and 180lbs psi boiler pressure were given names and included in the new "King Arthur" class of 4-6-0s designed by R E L Maunsell. His new engines had 200lbs psi boiler pressure and long travel valves and were capable of a very occasional ninety mile an hour sprint.

The elegant Edwardian locomotives were robust to a fault. During the 1914 - 1918 war a large number of 2-8-0 heavy freight locomotives designed by J G Robinson for the Great Central Railway were shipped to Europe together with sixty-nine Great Western Dean goods 0-6-0, and their simple strengths proved invaluable under the terrible operating conditions.

In 1922 Raven and Gresley both produced a three cylindered "Pacific" for their respective railways, the North Eastern and the Great Northern. Raven's "Pacific" was old fashioned with a high parallel boiler, inside Stephenson's valve gears and a firebox area inadequate for the tube length. Gresley's "Pacific" had outside Walschaerts valve gear operating the inside valve through a conjugating system. There was very little to oil up under the boiler. Although Gresley's "A1" was more modern it only fulfilled its potential after it had been altered as a result of lessons learned from comparison with a Great Western "Castle".

**BELOW** Gresley's A1 Pacific of 1922 only realised its full potential after being modified

# Chapter 11

# Grouping

THE RAILWAY EXECUTIVE COMMittee had been formed prior to 1914 in order to make the best use of the railway system during the first World War. This committee combined the talents of the general managers of the railways during and after the War until 1921. In 1923 over 120 separate railway companies amalgamated into four groups, later known as the 'Big Four', which were to retain their identity until Nationalisation in 1948. The largest of these groups was the London Midland and Scottish Railway, followed by the London and North Eastern Railway, the Great Western Railway and then the Southern Railway which was the smallest of all. The locomotive development policies reflected the tendency of each of the respective CMEs to follow tried and tested formulae where the resulting engines had proved to be economic

machines. For the GWR, C B Collett, who had taken over at Swindon after Churchward's retirement in 1921, continued the enlargement of a basic theme with the "Castle" class built in 1924. These engines had four cylinders set out to the 'Swindon taste' and 225 lbs boiler pressure. On 2nd May 1925 No 4074 Caldicote Castle hauling the 'Cornish Riviera' express ran the 225.7 miles from Paddington to Plymouth in 231.58 minutes with driver Rowe and fireman Cook in the cab. The locomotive did the job at between 19% and 20% cutoffs, and for each pound of coal that Cook threw on the fire ten pounds of water turned to steam. You cannot get much better than

that! In fact that sort efficiency would not be possible without first class Welsh coal which is 90% carbon.

The name of the train gives a clue to the 'luxury theme' of this chapter. Railway travellers were to be tempted away from travel by road by the promise of speed and comfort on the way to exotic places. The inclusion of 'Riviera' in the title of the train put the passenger in mind of a journey to the south of France. Another crack GWR express was the 'Cheltenham Flyer' which ran at an average speed of seventy miles per hour and was claimed to be 'The Fastest Train in the World'. A further ruse practised by the wily GWR publicists was to

assert that their "Castle"s were the 'most powerful class of locomotive in Britain'. Tractive effort, which is what this claim was all about, is a figure arrived at by doing sums that take into account the number of cylinders, their size, 85% of the boiler pressure and the driving wheel diameter in inches. At the end of a bit of complicated multiplication and division the tractive effort of the "Castle"s was calculated to be 31,625 lbs. This publicity, together with the comparison of the GWR 4-6-0 with and LNER 4-6-2 at the 1924 Wembley Exhibition sent a widening ripple across the placid pond of British locomotive design.

**ABOVE** The Cornish Riviera express was so named to give a sense of luxury

**CENTRE** The Castle class dates back to 1924. This is No 4096, Highclere Castle

The LNER CME was the Crewe-trained engineer Nigel Gresley, who had followed the design principles laid out by Ivatt when he built his celebrated large boilered "Atlantic"s. The main drawback of a four coupled design is the lack of adhesion on slippery rails. While keeping the essential proportions of the "Atlantic" Gresley added two more driving wheels and created a fine looking "Pacific", but with a boiler pressure of only 180lbs, its tractive effort was calculated to be 29,835lbs. At the Wembley Exhibition the large and racy "Pacific" stood next to a rather small engine around which the 'pressmen' hovered because it was billed as Britain's 'most powerful' locomotive.

The LNER countered with the argument that 'power' depended on boiler capacity. Tractive effort only represented the maximum pull possible, and if the engine's boiler was too small the tractive effort would fall off as the boiler pressure dropped. The LNER "Pacific" had the larger boiler and would therefore develop more 'horsepower' at high speeds when a small boiler would tend to become 'winded'. The argument was settled by comparative trials between the two designs in 1925. Driver Young of Old Oak Common was in charge of GWR No 4079 Pendinnis Castle during the runs on LNER metals that proved the superiority of the Great Western engine. Subsequently, Gresley increased the boiler pressure of his "Pacific" and lengthened the valve travel, enabling the design to realise its full potential at short cut off.

The LMS were likewise influenced when No 5000 Launceston Castle again proved her superiority during similar trials on their metals in 1926. To alleviate an obvious problem contact was made with the Southern Railway design team at Ashford, who had incorporated the principle of long travel valves in their latest design of 4-6-0, the "Lord Nelson"s, which had a tractive effort of 33,590 lbs. Plans of the new design were made available to the LMS which resulted in the creation of Henry Fowler's "Royal Scot" class in 1927. These engines broke through the Midland 'small engines' policy, though despite a shockingly modern short chimney they retained an old fashioned appearance with their very

**LEFT** The Royal Scot class was introduced in 1927, breaking the LMS policy of small engines

'Midland Railway' squareness of style. Later, we shall see how ex-GWR William Stanier, the new CME for the LMS, would improve matters further.

As for the "Lord Nelson" class, experience showed that despite the higher tractive effort the engines were not a great improvement (apart from a smoother ride) over the "King Arthur"s. It was the old argument of tractive effort versus boiler performance, and the "Lord Nelson"s could be finicky for steam. Using Welsh coal, I have fired to "King"s "Castle"s and "Lord Nelson"s and have found that the Great Western engines

steamed more reliably. I believe that on the "Lord Nelson" the brick arch was not at a steep enough angle to the firebars and thus firemen could not keep a sufficient depth of fuel over the centre back of the grate. This problem did not arise with hard, long flame coal.

To counter the new 'most powerful' challenge from the Southern Railway, Swindon produced an enlarged 4-6-0 with a long firebox, longer piston stroke, higher boiler pressure (250lbs) and smaller driving wheels. The mathematics of this combination gave the new engine a tractive effort of 40,300lbs. Named after British kings of the realm, this new Great Western class of locomotives was actually born out of a publicity war.

The travelling public were being offered increasingly luxurious, attractively designed and exotically named trains, hauled by locomotives that became household names for their power and speed. Pullman car trains ran on the Southern from Victoria to the continental ports. The Golden Arrow headboard and insignia graced locomotive 'front ends' on both sides of the Channel. The 'Bournemouth Belle' ran out of Waterloo, the 'Queen of Scots'

**OPPOSITE** Lord Nelson class could be tricky to fire says the author

**BELOW** Princess Elizabeth, shown here in later double-chimney form, averaged 70mph from Euston to Glasgow in 1936

**ABOVE** Duchess of Hamilton, a Coronation Class engine, originally had a streamlined casing

from King's Cross to Edinburgh. Eventually streamlined coaches hauled by streamlined locomotives, with record speeds being attained and surpassed, were run by both the LNER and the LMS as the two companies vied for the Anglo-Scottish traffic as their predecessors had barely forty years before. The 'Race to the North' was on again.

The round-topped boilers of Doncaster were competing against the Belpaire boilers of Crewe. William Stanier, recruited from his position as assistant to Collett on the GWR in 1931, was finally able to change the 'small engine' policy of the Midland dominated LMS. His predecessors, Hughes and Fowler, had not been so lucky. In 1933

Stanier's first "Princess" class "Pacific" No 6200 Princess Royal was built at Crewe. Bearing some resemblance to a GWR "King", she had a wider firebox with a pony truck underneath. The layout of the four cylinders was identical to the "King"s but with four sets of Walschaerts valve gears operating the piston valves. In 1936 No 6201 Princess Elizabeth hauled seven coaches non stop the 401 miles from Euston to Glasgow at an average speed of seventy miles per hour. Driver Laurie Earl on 'improved' "Pacific" No 6206 hauled sixteen coaches weighing 500 tons from Euston to Rugby, covering the 82.6 miles in 83.4 minutes.

In 1937 larger boilered "Pacific"s with six foot nine inch driving wheels were produced to Stanier's design. Initially named "Coronation"s and later known as the "Duchess" class, they were originally built with streamlined casings painted blue with white striping that matched the design of the 'Coronation Scot' train. Built with larger fireboxes than the "Princesses", they had the same boiler pressure and larger driving wheels giving them a tractive effort of 40,000 lbs. Only two sets of Walschaerts valve gears were fitted, these were outside the frames and operated the inside valves through rocker arms in a reversal of the method used on

the Great Western "Kings". To help the fireman a steam operated coal pusher was fitted in the tender.

The "Duchess" class had been built at a time of intense competition between the LMSR's west and the LNER's east coast routes to the north. In 1934 Gresley's improved "Pacific" No 4472 Flying Scotsman was timed at 100 mph. Then the streamlined "A4" no 2509 Silver Link hauling the 'Silver Jubilee' streamlined express topped 112.5 mph down Stoke bank. On 29th June 1937 LMS "Pacific" No 6220 Coronation hauling the eight

**BELOW** No 6220 Coronation reached a speed of 114mph in 1937

coaches of the 'Coronation Scot' express reached 114mph just two miles outside Crewe. They had to stop at Crewe! There were 20mph speed restrictions on the approach as set by the signalmen. With the brakes full on they were still doing 105mph with one mile to go. At 56mph they went over the 20mph pointwork without coming off the rails and succeeded in coming safely to rest in the platform at Crewe station. It was obvious that this had been an exuberant and hazardous attempt at the speed record which, while successful, could have had terrible consequences. Express locomotives do not have to have strong brakes as the train stops the locomotive. There were only twelve brake blocks on the 164 ton "Pacific" and there were sixteen brake blocks to each thirty ton coach. Drivers were instructed not to exceed sixty miles per hour when running 'light engine' i.e. with no coaches. The 'Coronation Scot' and its locomotive had a total weight of 434 tons, 164 tons of which were inadequately braked at speeds above sixty miles per hour. I doubt that the outcome would have been the same under modern track maintenance regimes.

With the long descent from Stoke offering their trains plenty of space the LNER set a record that the LMS could not top. In July 1938 Joseph Duddington drove the streamlined "A4" Mallard up to a speed of 126mph on a special 'brake test' run. This record has never been beaten by a steam locomotive.

An interesting practical comment

here. It is not difficult to make a locomotive go extremely fast. It is quite difficult to make them go faster than 100 miles per hour plus the figure you are aiming to exceed. Speed settles on a plateau, there is no precise formula or setting of controls that will ensure a given speed. Locomotives have a natural galloping action, though some run more freely than others. The space ahead is swallowed up amazingly quickly while the driver tries a shorter cutoff, finds no increase in speed, then tries a longer cutoff. Has the speedo reacted? If it has not another mile has flashed beneath the wheels during his thirty five seconds of indecision.

There were no further challenges to be met from the LMSR.

The Southern did not go in for record breaking high speed exploits. However, the air-smoothed "Pacific"s designed by O V S Bulleid in 1941, which were fitted with his chain driven miniature Walschaerts valve gear operating in an oil bath, were capable of topping 100 miles per hour and did so right up to the final days of steam on the Southern in 1967.

A world war soon ended those exciting summertime races. Competitive displays of finery became no more than memories that warmed the spirits through the grey years ahead.

**LEFT** Mallard still holds the record for the fastest steam locomotive, at 126mph

# Chapter 12

# World War II

WILLIAM STANIER'S ASSISTANT from 1933, Robert Riddles, had immense practical experience of the problems that fitters and engine crews faced in their daily tasks. He had been present on the footplates of the LMS "Pacific"s when they were road tested in 1935 and also during the record long distance trials of 16 November 1936, and the high speed runs of June 1937. He had acted as fireman and driver during the "Coronation Scot"s tour of America in 1939. He had coped with hot axle boxes, melted cross head slippers, collapsed brick arches and poor coal. It is doubtful that any other man had brought so much useful experience to the job of designing steam locomotives. At the outbreak of war in 1939, Robert Riddles was given the job of heading the Directorate of Transportation Equipment. The Great

Western Dean goods 0-6-0s of 1883 had once again been sent to Europe earlier that year. In 1941 he sent 91 Robinson 2-8-0s to the Middle East, all of which were to remain there. The urgent need for heavy goods engines for Britain's war effort was met by a large order for Stanier 2-8-0s. Brighton works produced one of these a week, they built 93 in all. Two hundred and eight of these engines were built for the War Department, most of which went to the Middle East after Europe had been overrun by the Germans.

Because Stanier's locomotives were fairly sophisticated they required scarce materials and time to build them. Riddles designed an 'Austerity' engine that was cheaper to make. The North British Locomotive Company in Glasgow had built the Fowler 'Royal Scot's, and with their co-operation

Riddles worked out a simple design. For cheapness and ease of construction, Riddles gave them round topped, parallel boilers, and he substituted cheaper metals for some of the castings. They had outside Walschaerts valve gear, two cylinders, boiler pressure of 225lbs and a narrow grate. The cab and footplates were very plain with no frills. The first of these engines came out in January 1943. It had taken ten days to put together and five months had elapsed from the placement of the order. The North British built them at the rate of five per week, 935 in total being built, with 450 lent to the four railway companies until the engines were needed overseas. The design was a great success.

An engine was later requested with an axle loading of only 13.5 tons. Riddles decided on a 2-10-0. He made the tread of the centre driving wheel wide but flangeless. This enabled the locomotive to run through four and a half chain curves without excessive friction. These engines were given wide fireboxes of forty square feet. However, the war had ended before the first of the 150 such

engines ordered were built by the North British Locomotive Company. A large number of shunting engines based on a Hunslett- designed saddle tank were also produced for the War Department. These engines were strong but simple, and strong but simple continued to be the theme of the subsequent locomotives designed by Riddles that we will get to meet in the next chapter.

On his return to the LMS at the end of the war, R A Riddles was appointed vice president (Engineering) of the company.

CENTRE Over 100 Stanier 2-8-0s were built for the War Department

BELOW Riddles designed a simple to build engine for the War Department

# Chapter 13

# Nationalisation & BR Standard Locomotives

IN JANUARY 1948 THE FOUR RAILWAY companies were taken over by the government, and British Railways was created. Compensation was paid to the shareholders. The former CMEs,

Peppercorn, Bulleid, Hawksworth and Ivatt, were replaced by R A Riddles, who was made the mechanical and electrical engineer responsible to the newly created railway executive. Riddles had started out as an apprentice on the LNWR at Crewe in 1909, and had worked his way up as we saw in the previous chapter, to vice president (Engineering) of the LMS. His flair for organisation and design were now to be tested as he worked to combine the skills and temperaments of the four railway locomotive design teams.

Locomotive design on the Great Western had been stagnant for many years. On the Southern, Bulleid was

seen to be going off on a tangent with his "Leader" project, and Peppercorn on the North Eastern was developing his large modernised "Pacific"s which, however, retained the traditional Doncaster round topped firebox. The LMS under Ivatt had thoroughly embraced labour saving innovations, for example, self cleaning smoke boxes and fully rocking grates with hopper ashpans. The Ivatt 2-6-0s and 2-6-2 tanks were very up to date though small machines that replaced the ancient 0-6-0s formerly in service.

CMEs usually relied on their chief draughtsmen to do the detail work on proposed new locomotive projects. The name of the CME that produced the design often hid the name of the man or men that gave actual shape to the locomotive in question, thereby making it recognisable as the CME's style. So it was with Riddles, who brought together the chief draughtsmen of Derby, Swindon, Brighton and Doncaster in order to discuss and give advice for the new range of Standard locomotives suitable for all line usage. Of course, the ex-LNWR Crewe apprentice could not resist having almost all of Britain's locomotive fleet painted black. The locomotive trials of September 1948 were used to test the strengths and weaknesses of the engines then available, the results of which revealed no great differences.

The largest of the proposed classes

was a Class 8 "Pacific" and the smallest some Class 3 2-6-2 tanks. The year 1948 was one during which the British economy was under great strain, the winter was a hard one and the effects of the last war were still very evident. Ration books were still being used in 1951. I remember that as a shift worker I was entitled to an extra two ounces of cheese on my ration book for sandwiches for work. Riddles published the comparative costs of building steam locomotives as opposed to diesel or electric locomotives. Electric locos were double the cost, plus the cost of the lineside power supply, and diesels were four times the cost of steam. The coal fields of Britain were very accessible but oil had to be imported, and hydro-elec-

tric power supplies were not an option. So it was that in January 1951 a brand new very American looking 'Pacific' locomotive made its appearance, and was named Britannia. Riddles and his team were clever. The new machine was different enough not to be an example of any of the previous main line express engines. To suit the austerity of the time the engine was designated a 'mixed traffic' locomotive. She was a Class 7 and had features that were culled from the best practices of the four constituent railways. One could see elements of the North Eastern in the slide bars and valve gear and the boiler and frames were Bulleid. The smokebox and many of the cab fittings, including window catches, were from the very practical designs of Swindon. The reverser, though working fore and aft like a grocer's bacon slicer, had the gearing of an LMS loco and the regulator handle, like that of a Bulleid or GN 'Pacific' was the pull-out kind. The clean, uncluttered backhead was more like a Western or a North Eastern loco than an LMS design. On an LMS loco it is difficult to clean the backhead as closely packed hot and intrusive control valves scorch the wrists of unwary enginemen.

Riddles had achieved this by giving aspects of the design to the draughtsmen of Brighton, Derby, Swindon and Doncaster. The Britannia was built at Crewe and with fourteen others of the class were sent to work on the Great Eastern line out of Liverpool Street, and a further ten went to the GWR.

**BELOW** Britannia was a modern and clever design, and the first Class 7 Pacific

The truly innovative features included no fall plate between the engine and tender, which gave a firm base on which to stand when firing. The cab was supported on cantilevers off the back of the boiler so that the fit of the cab was tighter and less draughty than on previous designs which had to allow for the expansion and contraction of the boiler in and out of the cabs. Regulator rodding was external to the boiler so that glands were not made too tight by the attempts to prevent drips and blows into the cab. There were small windows in the tender front for dust free backwards running and quite

good seats too. But they were essentially very simple locomotives: only two cylinders, no steam operated reversers, no electric lighting, and back to the old oil lamps for Southern and North Eastern crews who had become used to better illumination.

One modern feature that had been tried on the LMS by Ivatt was the fitting of roller bearings to the axles. This made the engine very free running indeed! The handbrake, which was an LMS bevelled gear design and never very efficient, had to be forced on very hard or the engine toddled off when its crew had parked it in the shed.

The roller bearings, curiously enough, make these engines hard and noisy to ride on. There is no give on the hard steel rollers. The 9F produced later has old fashioned white metalled axle boxes and the ride is quieter and softer than that of a "Britannia".

Predictably, Great Western crews compared the new locomotives unfavourably with their own designs. They found them noisy and draughty, they complained that the coal was blown off the shovel because there was no fall plate; this was despite the fact that Great Western tender locos have no cab doors! All Western locos are fired from the left side of the cab, the firemen fire right handed. The Standard locos, like every other engine built since 1940, were fired left handed from the right side of the cab, and drivers sat where most station platforms and signals are, on the left. The Western men said that their backs hurt when they shovelled from a shovel plate instead of from two inches lower

**BELOW** A rebuilt Southern 'West Country' class 4-6-2

than their boots as they had done before. They did not get on with the technique needed in order to get coal into the back corners of the wide firebox. On Western locos the fireboxes are quite narrow, though long, and the Western shovel had a very long blade which was filled to excess before whacking the coal through the firehole door. They did not have to aim, just whack. Now they had to twist that great blade to one side or the other, and it was not easy for them. They also complained that the smoke deflectors obscured the driver's view forward. It should be noted that Great Western engines, having sharply tapered boilers with the taper on the top, give the driver an extremely good forward view and have never needed smoke deflectors to lift the steam. The new engine's boiler was tapered at the bottom which did not give as good a view forward.

Elsewhere, crews were happy with the new design, which was seen as a fairly primitive substitute for existing multi-cylindered express locos, and a vast improvement on some of the 4-6-0s of the Great Eastern section of the Eastern region. Speeds of over ninety miles per hour were to be recorded behind

"Britannia" "Pacific"s. Preparation and disposal duties were made easy by the lack of inside valve gears, the roller bearings and rocking and drop grates. Strangely, the self-cleaning smokebox did not work with the Welsh coal burned at Nine Elms. The excessively dusty coal which filled our tenders went straight through the tubes only partly burned, and piled up against the mesh so that it was almost up to the top of the door and had to be shovelled out by hand or the engine would not steam next trip.

This also happened on the class 5 4-6-0s that were built at Doncaster to replace the old "King Arthur"s, and which even took the names of some of the Urie "Arthur"s. The class 5s were fast and strong. Like all BR Standard locos they lost their zip if the boiler pressure went below 200lbs. They were essentially a Stanier "Black 5" with modern features. The roller bearings made them harsh and rattly to work on. They did not steam as well on Welsh dust as our "King Arthur"s did, so we had some worrying moments. I discovered, after firing on a "Castle" to Plymouth, that if you filled the box ridiculously high with a great 'haycock', like a "Castle", and kept whacking the stuff in over the half door, steaming could be improved.

**OPPOSITE** Women who had learned boiler shop skills were to lose their jobs in the post-war Swindon works

**BELOW** A Standard Class 4 4-6-0 in a typical British Railways' station

The smaller class 4 4-6-0s were not as popular as the class 5s because when running at speed the tender would try to overtake the engine. The fore and aft movement caused by the pistons was magnified by slack drawbar buffers. Coal would shuffle out of the coal hatch and rattle noisily onto the steel footplate. Eventually someone earned themselves a £25.00 prize for suggesting that a coal door flap be fitted, they did not run freely or steam very well and double chimneys were fitted to many of the Southern based engines. The mostly steel footplate was a feature of Standard locos that contributed to the noise and coldness of the cabs.

BELOW The Class 4 4-6-0 was not popular with drivers because it was cold and noisy

The 2-6-4 class 4 tanks that were built at Brighton were based on a Stanier design and were extremely good. They were used to replace elderly 4-4-2 tanks on short distance passenger work. They rode as smoothly as a coach. They did not have roller bearings. They were as easy to drive in reverse as they were chimney first, and it is difficult to see why Bulleid was so convinced that the double ended "Leader" would be any improvement on a modern 2-6-4 tank which could handle intensive passenger services, in and out of termini, with ease.

The smallest of the BR Standard designs were not disguised by having

Continental/American style running plates, but were as Ivatt had made them for the LMS. These were fine, practical locomotives and they became everyone's favourite. The detail work for the very popular heavy goods loco, the class 9F 2-10-0, was done by Jarvis at Brighton. These engines ran smoothly and faster than might be expected bearing in mind their massive cylinders and five foot driving wheels. The boiler was pitched as high as the loading gauge would permit in order that a wide firebox could be put over the trailing driving wheel and still be deep enough to hold the depth of fire required to withstand the pull of the exhaust. As a result, some of the boiler fittings, dome, mudhole door clamps etc are pared down so as to clear tunnels and bridges. With such a small dome it became apparent that water could enter the regulator valve if the boiler was filled to the normal level. The water gauges were given false "top nuts" that partially obscured the top third of the glass, so that firemen had only filled the glass two thirds though

it appeared to be full. When water enters the regulator it can result in an uncontrollable slip; this once happened under a footbridge on which children were standing. The blast from the chimney blew out the planking and the children fell to their deaths.

The 9Fs were made very flexible, despite the five driving axles, by the same method that Riddles had used on his WD 2-10-0s of World War Two. The centre driving wheels had no flange and could roll 'steam roller like' across the head of the rail on tight curves. Like the "Crab" 4-6-0s of the LMS, the cylinders being of a large diameter were inclined

steeply at the leading end so as to give sufficient clearance when entering curving platforms.

Because of the driving wheels below the firebox the ashpan is also shallow at its outer edges and so limiting the flow of air to the edges of the fire. The firebed is only six inches in depth when the coal is level with the bottom of the fire door ring. With a heavy load and with Welsh coal the fire needed to be up to the level of the top of the door opening to make these engines steam. This I found out when my fireman was puzzled that the engine was not steaming with the fire at a height usually carried on our Bulleid "Pacific"s. He then doubled the depth and it worked, and we had no more trouble.

The missing Class 8 Standard 4-6-2 was built in 1954 as a result of the terrible collision that took place at Harrow in December 1952. This had involved three trains and destroyed three locomotives, one of which was the newly rebuilt Turbomotive renamed Princess Anne.

I took my first look at this impressive machine at the International Railway Congress exhibition. It was about the same size as a "Merchant Navy" and had three cylinders that were supplied steam by the Caprotti valve gear. This undramatic gear looks like propshafts on a large car, for instance there is no little 'dance' of the combination lever, no rocking of the expansion links as a result of the ducking and diving of return cranks and eccentric rods. Its poppet valves separate the events that give 'cut off' from the event that opens up the exhaust route to the chimney.

In comparison with the "Britannia"s which have a firebox of a similar size to a "West Country", Duke of Gloucester (the new engine's name) had a firebox with the grate area of a "Merchant Navy", i.e. 48.5 square feet. Everything else was typical of the Standard locomotives that were already in service. However, the new engine was never popular with its crews. It was unlikely to be the equivalent of the mighty four cylindered "Duchesses", though it should have been as good as a good three cylindered rebuilt "Royal Scot". It is highly probable that as it was the only engine of its type, no-one ever got used to driving it. But more of this engine later.

**BELOW** The LMS Turbomotive used turbines instead of cylinders

# Chapter 14

# Steam in Decline 1954 to 1968

THE CONSERVATIVE GOVERNMENT of 1954 decided that steam power had to go. It may have been seen as a symbol of the "socialist" nationalisation of railways that had taken place in 1948. Under this nationalisation the management had publicly declared their support for steam.

I was doing my National Service at this time and will never forget the dismay that I felt on reading in the Sunday newspapers the coming end of steam traction on Britain's railways. At nineteen years of age I had been a fireman at Nine Elms when I was called up, now it seemed that I would have no job to return to at the end of my army service. I was "Gloomy Groomey" that day! The decline of steam will therefore be a somewhat personal account.

Luckily for me the changeover to diesel and electric traction was not to be finally accomplished until 1968. In the meantime I was able to experience the declining years of steam on the footplates of most of the great express locomotive classes that were hauling trains north, south, east and west during that period. At the age of thirty I was delighted to find myself a driver in number three link at Nine Elms, which involved runs to Bournemouth and Salisbury, and boat trains to Southampton docks. During this period I was therefore driving examples of Bulleid's original "Pacific"s and comparing them to the rebuilt engines as modified by the Brighton drawing office under Jarvis.

The decline of steam was to be more prolonged than was forecast in 1954. The five express diesel locomotives, two of them LMS designs by Ivatt, the other three Southern designs by Bulleid, had been allocated to the Southern Region for a short time before being transferred to the Midland Region. As a result, contrary to simple logic the most "modern", i.e. the most electrified railway, retained

**ABOVE** At the controls of a 1950s diesel engine

**OPPOSITE** Britains first main line diesel train leaving St Pancras for a test run to Derby and Manchester. The locomotive's designer HA Ivatt is climbing on board

**ABOVE** The author spent time driving Merchant Navy engines

express steam services on its South Western section, long after the "less modern" railways had gone over to diesel or electric traction.

Before I left the army I was privileged to meet Bill Hoole of King's Cross, and he, knowing how I missed the footplate life, (as the Army had decided that a fireman would be better used as a lorry driver) provided me with his roster months ahead. This was so that I could ride with

him on the North Eastern "Pacific"s to Grantham and Newcastle. The "Deltic"s were now taking over some of the duties and I was delighted at the opportunity to learn more of my craft on the fine "Pacific"s that would soon be displaced forever. Bill's regular engine at the time was No 60007 Sir Nigel Gresley, but it was on No 60008 Dwight D Eisenhower that I had my first memorable trip.

It was on 19 April 1955 when I fired the

ABOVE A diesel train pulling out of a very wet Marylebone Station, London in 1960

10.40am King's Cross to Peterborough while Bill's mate took a break back in the train. The corridor tender enabled this swap to take place. Later, at Grantham, we had some food before taking over the engine which had been turned and serviced. The train that we now headed was the up Flying Scotsman which had arrived fifteen minutes late.

The "A4"s are a 'powerpack' enclosed in a small and graceful shape. Within the cab the low footplate with its raised floorboards to the left and right of the firing level, accentuates the height of the backhead. The water gauges are above the average man's head and you climb up to the driver's bucket seat. This is in contrast to Southern "Pacific"s where you stand higher up the boiler and the cab roof is nearer to your head. Externally though, an "A4" seems no larger than a "West Country".

one miles per hour at Essendine (timed from the train) with the boiler pressure down a little at 200lbs.

In contrast to the Southern methods on Bulleid's engines, the water was seldom more than halfway up the glass and the firebed was so thin that its surface 'danced' under the exhaust blast. We arrived in King's Cross (after suffering two signal checks and observing the speed restriction through Peterborough) two minutes early! I was stone deaf when I got off the engine after 101 minutes of incredible noise. Within the cab Bill and his mate relaxed again, a job well done. The hot engine smelled of scorched metal as the firedoor cooled off, and every pin on the valve gear exuded the aroma of warm rape oil. Like a thoroughbred horse 60008 stood with her nose to the buffers while I took a last admiring gaze.

As a result of trips like this I modified my firing technique on the rebuilt "Merchant Navy" engines. They were fitted with baffle plates as the steam operated firedoor mechanism had been taken off. The baffle plate made it very difficult to keep a really deep fire at the back of the box. Most firemen would not put the baffle in. I reasoned that

Bill's fireman made up his fire a little and we were off. The power displayed over the next hundred miles was blood tingling! Bill worked her on full regulator and at 'cut offs' ranging from between 35% up hill and 12% on the level. We reached a top speed of ninety where a baffle was supplied, non usage could be used to deny compensation for scalding if a tube burst. I tried the shallow fire I had seen used on the "A4"s and "A3"s and it worked. And I could do it with the baffle in place. However, this resulted in many long faces on the firemen that took over from me at Salisbury. It was years later that I realised that the evil smelling oil that often drenched the hot firedoors of the engines I took over on the up trains to London were an attempt to "punish" me for not handing over box-fulls of fire to them on the down trains!

The "West Country"s really did like great haycock fires just inside the door, and this was the coolest way to fire them as no heat could escape into the smallish cab. I could make them steam when I had to on six inches of firebed when the coal was 100% dust, by feeding the white hot bed with dust sprayed off the shovel like the mechanical stoker on an American "Big Boy". Bulleid "Pacific" No 34018 loved this treatment as did 35018. Meanwhile on the Western Region nothing had changed since Churchward's day, and engines were always fired with great haycock fires and to excellent effect. This I was to discover

when I rode on No 6012 King Edward VI from Paddington to Plymouth (225.7 miles) on Friday 27 June 1958. We had a load of nine coaches and a van. The train was the 9.30am semi-fast and its crew came from Old Oak Common shed.

The safety valves were sizzling and shushing within their brass housing as we departed four minutes late, but they

BELOW Creating a good fire is key to a succesfully running engine

Although the "King"s have an eleven foot six inch firebox the high brick arch and steeply sloping grate allows a fireman to feed the fuel in mainly to the centre and the rear of the box. The heaped fuel, however, works its way forward to keep sufficient firebed depth at the front tubeplate.

There was no shovel plate. The tender floor from which Dai lifted the coal was inches lower than the wooden footplate of the engine. When he had scooped a very full shovel of coal, Dai pulled open the firedoor flap by the chain attached. It would land with a thump on the boards. He then swung the coal into the centre of the box and replaced the flap before sticking the shovel back under the coal in the tender for the next delivery.

This may sound a painfully elaborate way to fire an engine. However, the timing becomes perfect and minimal effort is expended by an experienced man. I fired from Taunton to Newton Abbot, about fifty miles, and soon got into the "swing of it". The engine rode smoothly and the absence of doors did not make for a draughty cab, though I noticed that GWR engine men wore their jackets tucked inside their overall trousers, and they wore cycle clips above their

became quiet as the pressure dropped back. The haycock fire was not properly alight but fireman, Dai Lloyd, gave it a lift up with a heavy dart and she steamed easily after that with steady and unhurried firing.

boots – to keep out the dust I supposed. The four cylindered loco had quite a bark at the chimney, but with Welsh coal and the heavy fire no destruction of the firebed was apparent.

I was impressed. The cab was always kept spotlessly clean. Both men worked well together and kindly warned me to put a little extra fuel in just before we ran along the sea wall at Dawlish, where the views could be stunning. We arrived at Plymouth right on time and later that evening I joined Dai and his driver in the Liara Inn. It was full of Welsh enginemen who sang beautifully all evening as we drank away the thirst that only engines can create. At 07.00am next morning, with a slight hangover, I joined my friends in the cab of "Castle" class No 7031, Cromwell's Castle for the return trip to London. We had a load of six coaches to Newton Abbot, then twelve on to Paddington. And again the engine did the job nicely. I noted the cabs were painted green inside and did not rattle around the boiler. The engines held their water and did not prime when their water was at the top of the glass. We never had to set back in order to start away from stations.

**BELOW** These are two examples of express engines the author used to drive. In front is 35004 Cunard White Star, an unrebuilt Bulleid Pacific. Behind is a rebuilt version of the same class

**ABOVE** 35027 Port Line is another engine the author used to drive. It weighed 100 tons – without its tender!

A month later I tried this method of firing on BR Standard 5 4-6-0 73088. My regular mate Len Rickard and I were working a one hundred and seven mile non stop special of ten coaches from Bournemouth to Waterloo. The engine loved that kind of firing. Our passengers gave us a pound each at the end of the trip, my wages then were about ten pounds per week including 'mileage'.

On 30 December 1957 I joined driver Brown and fireman Whittingham in the cab of 8P 46233, Duchess of Sutherland at the head of the mid-day 'Scot'. We had a load of fourteen coaches equalling 469 tons and a tight eighty-minute schedule for the eighty miles to Rugby. The coal mainly consisted of large slabs of hard which spat and crackled from the brimming firebox door. It sounded like a fish and chip fryer as the

Heat spalled the slate like coal. These large locomotives have quite small cabs and the height of their footplates is a complete contrast to the low footplates of North Eastern engines. My head was often out in the rain and ash when I stood behind the driver, keeping out of the fireman's way as he swung great slabs of coal to right and left back corners of the wide firebox. The boiler pressure, which had been at 240lbs, soon fell to 200 and stayed there all the way to Rugby. The fireman was 'up against it' as the engine primed with only half a glass of water. She was not in the best of health. The engine rode well, though, and the cab was not dusty. The driver, sitting on the left, could reach his controls easily and the brake valve, unlike those on the Great Western Kings, could be operated while sitting down and leaning out of the open window. The long regulator handle closed itself frequently and it was common practice to jam a piece of coal in the quadrant to keep it wide open on the fast stretches.

As was usual on the LMR, the side windows were dirty enough to be mistaken for metal. The shovel plate was almost on the floor, the fall plate between the loco and tender was humped and divided into two parts. The ten ton capacity coal space was cavernous and a steam operated coal pusher was demonstrated to me and a wall of coal pressed against the tender front.

At Crewe, my companions went off with their engine and 46202 Princess Mary Louise

backed onto the train with two extra coaches, making sixteen in all, equal to 550 tons. The "Princess" was more like a large Great Western engine. It had a smaller square fronted and somewhat draughty cab. Away we went, two more Crewe men at the controls, 250lbs on

**BELOW** At night, the shed lighting beautifully illuminates a West Country swathed in a wreath of smoke and steam

the boiler and full regulator with seldom less than 30% cut off. We just scraped over Shap after being stopped at Oxenholme. I had a spell firing as the engine slipped and struggled as we breasted the summit at walking pace. The driver had also had a go on the shovel. The pressure was down to 180lbs, and we ran down to Carlisle with both injectors on for a long time

as the water level in the boiler had become very low.

We were an hour late away from Carlisle and had the assistance of a banker over Beattock. During this leg of the journey both the baffle plate and the protector ring fell into the fire and melted, adding to the dross on the firebars. We arrived at Glasgow at 10.55pm. I was very black and tired after nine and a half hours and four hundred miles on the footplate. I was assured that this had been an unusually bad run.

I returned to Euston the next evening on the 09.25pm in the cab of English Electric diesel 10001, which had doubled headed the thirteen-coach train with 10000. We went up Beattock at forty-five miles per hour and came down the other side at eighty. The brakes were twice as slow as on a steam locomotive, both in application and release. The fumes and lack of action also made me sleepy, but we arrived at Euston twenty minutes early.

Finally, a trip on the Great Eastern, thanks to Mr R H N Hardy, whom I had met while firing to Bert Hooker of locomotive exchange fame. It was 1958, diesels were being introduced on this region in increasing numbers. I joined Stratford men on "Britannia" "Pacific" 70040 Clive of India at the head of ten coaches on the down 'Norfolkman' with one stop at Ipswich and then Norwich. The pressure soon dropped from 240

**ABOVE** A West Country at Eastleigh Works

rejoined the crew who had turned the engine and worked on the fire. We had five coaches on to Ely where the load was made up to ten coaches. I fired this return trip but overloaded the fire on the climb out of Cambridge, and I began to sweat as the pressure dropped to 200lbs. A slightly lighter fire improved matters considerably and we had 220lbs the rest of the way, arriving at Liverpool Street two minutes early. The ride was harsh for a "Pacific", and noisy. The crew were ready to 'go for it' when they could, making it an interesting and lively experience for me. Later, Mr Hardy quizzed me on what I had learned while in possession of the footplate pass he had issued to me.

Back at Nine Elms main line trains were still being hauled by the elderly "King Arthur"s and "Lord Nelson" 4-6-0s. One foggy day in February 1959, having worked "N15" 30784 to Southampton Docks, my driver suggested a tour around the works at Eastleigh which were handy to the loco shed in which we stabled our engine. We saw a "Lord Nelson" being fitted with a new copper firebox. In contrast, three "West Country"s (Braunton was one of them) were being rebuilt to conven-

lbs down to 200 and we had a rough time to Ipswich with water in the bottom of the glass. While we were stopped the fireman got her round a bit and he kept 200 on the clock to Norwich and we arrived right on time. At 2.40pm I tional style, and five "Merchant Navy"s were next in line. The rebuilt Bulleid "Pacific"s often appeared on the Sunday 10.54am Waterloo to Bournemouth, smelling strongly of paint. Gone were the days of a twenty-minute oil round, now it took an hour and a quarter to do three sets of Walschaerts valve gear and a bit of climbing up the high running plate to attend to other oilboxes. To my eye they looked better and the cabs were cooler with less hot pipework, and we could now see where we were going! Instead of having to throw out fifty square feet of fire with a long shovel (having first taken off the cab doors) we could now drop the clinker into a hopper ashpan and then into the pit. They rode harder than before because their springs were less flexible, and they had a

LEFT The author as a young man on 30851 Sir Francis Drake, on the day of his driving test at Basingstoke

tendency to develop a 'knock' at about thirty-five thousand miles. The resulting thumps and bangs made them seem reluctant gallopers until they were travelling at more than sixty miles per hour.

However, gallop they could! On 26 March 1959, driver Len Rickard and I were in charge of rebuilt "Merchant Navy" No 35017 Belgian Marine hauling the 11.05am non stop to Salisbury with a thirteen-coach train. We did the 83.8 miles in 77 minutes with a top speed of around 102mph down the bank from Grately.

During those 77 minutes, three thousand gallons of water were used, and I shovelled about two tons of coal through the firehole door.

On the 22 May 1959 I took my driving test on "Lord Nelson" No 30851 Sir Francis Drake. We had a good run, 10.54am out of Waterloo and right time to Basingstoke. A pint in the Railway Arms, then back to London on 75078. Inspector Pemberton got off at Woking and told me that I had passed. None of Len Rickard's firemen had ever failed. I was twenty-three years old and steam had just another eight years left before it ended on the Southern in 1967. During that period the number of steam locomotives working on the Southern declined from about 1200 to about 150, twenty-four of which were based at Nine Elms. The "Merchant Navy"s had all been rebuilt by the end of 1959, and

BELOW The A2, Blue Peter, is the sole survivor of 15 A2 class locomotives designed by Arthur Peppercorn of the LNER

of the pre-war Southern designs only Maunsell's "S15"s, a few 2-6-0s and 0-6-0s remained by the end of 1965. By 1966 we had just begun to become aware of the emptiness of the shed. In the 'autumn of steam' the 'leaves' fell so slowly that when I look today at photographs of the period I cannot remember that it looked so run down and empty.

In August 1966 "A2" No 60532 Blue Peter arrived from Scotland for an LCB special to Exeter. On Sunday the 14th I was booked to drive it as far as Salisbury. Although I had been looking forward to the trip from the start it did not go well. Because of a broken rail in the dip under the coal hopper we had trouble getting off shed on time. When the engine was warm enough to shut the cylinder cocks the middle set stayed open, - but we had to go! My fireman, C Collier, did his best, but a tender full of Welsh dust did not suit the engine at all. We only had a nine coach load and ought to have romped away. Several signal checks on the way to Basingstoke and an easy schedule masked the situation at first, but from Worting we were limping along with a dead fire and the centre cylinder cock still blowing hard. We had used 3000

gallons of water already and went over Grately with 100 lbs on the gauge and only a quarter of a glass of water. Black with dust and soaked in sweat we could only roll down the hill to Salisbury while we filled up the boiler. The crew that took over for the run to Exeter stopped for lack of steam on Honiton bank, they had done well to get that far. A North Eastern fireman had ridden with us; both he and I had tried our hands at firing but to no bet-

CENTRE Driver Len Rickard stands in front of No. 35005 Canadian Pacific before driving it to London at the head of the Bournemouth Belle. This engine was saved from the scrapyard and is still at work today.

ter effect. It had been a disappointing experience for I knew what she should have been capable of having fired "A3"s "A4"s and "A1"s to Bill Hoole on the Newcastle trips.

Looking at my logbooks for those final years when we represented the last main line steam line in Britain, I can see patterns that I had not noticed at the time. Duff trips and tough trips are recorded, then a note that said "We have been clearing out the old coal off

the ground around the 'triangle'". Old coal, mostly dust with some earth and weeds, its calorific content leached out by sun and rain. This was what my firemen were having to use when they made up the firebed prior to running light engine to Waterloo. Sometimes, while I was oiling up the engine, my mate in the cab would be struggling to find some lumpy coal to shovel. Two spare firemen, ankle deep in the dust in the tender, searched by hand for pieces of coal to throw to my fireman for his fire. It is on record that young Nine Elms drivers 'tore about a bit' in the final months of steam. Some of them were followed about night and day by enthusiasts that yearned to 'clock a ton'. The track had been re-laid for 90mph plus running for the new electric services. Those last days when every platform end held a throng of photographers will never be repeated. We were just doing our daily job. Steam locomotives today are operated as an 'out of the ordinary' event.

When the final steam engine left its train to run back to the shed and its crew went home, the crowds left the platforms and they did not bother to watch trains for the next ten years.

# Epilogue

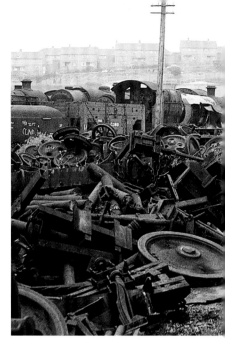

DESPITE THE BEST EFFORTS OF the 'modernisers' the history of steam does not end in 1968. Sent to the scrapyards in their hundreds many engines died under the cutter's torch. I remember watching No. 35004 Cunard White Star being sliced vertically like a piece of cake at Eastleigh depot. My mate and I had walked to the shed in driving rain after working the 5.30pm down from Waterloo on 7 February 1967. Four days later, on the same turn, I picked up the severed regulator handle from where it had dropped on the ground and carried it with me on the return working to London.

Two hundred dead engines lay in Barry Island. Pilgrimages were made to see them as reverently as the 'faithful' are wont to do for saintly relics. Driver Alan Wilton of Nine Elms moved heaven and earth to preserve an un-

CENTRE As steam was phased out around two hundred engines were sent to the scrapyard on Barry Island

ABOVE RIGHT Over the next twenty years most of these engines were purchased by restoration groups and preserved

BELOW RIGHT The complex restoration of the Duke of Gloucester was one of the most outstanding achievements of the preservation movement

rebuilt "West Country" No. 34023 Blackmoor Vale. Groups of enthusiasts began to organise themselves so they could purchase their own locomotives with the starry-eyed intention of returning them to steam. It was totally irrational, but today, almost forty years later, the results can be seen as proof that time cannot destroy that which has been constructed, only lack of interest can destroy these things.

The Duke of Gloucester has been rescued and reconstructed by a group

who were fascinated by its unique qualities. They have made her a more reliable performer in the process. On 1 June 1988, I sat in the spotless cab of rebuilt "Merchant Navy" No. 35027 Port Line. She had been restored in just five short years from a Barry wreck by a two hundred strong group who had raised £120,000 and learned many new skills in the process. I placed my hand on the warm regulator and felt an instant sense of empathy with the huge machine. It had been twenty-one years since I had last placed my hand on that regulator at the head of the 5.30pm Waterloo to Bournemouth in July 1967. With my fireman, Vic Spillett, we had maintained a steady eighty miles per hour during the journey. A new "A1" "Pacific" is under construction as I write, and a new generation is falling under the spell of the iron horse.

The history of steam is still being made.

**Bibliography:**

*A History of the Growth of the Steam Engine* - Robert H Thurston A. M. C. E

*The Development of the Locomotive* - Clement E Stretton

*The British Steam Railway Locomotive 1825 - 1925* - E L Ahrons

*British Steam Since 1900* - W A Tuplin DrSc, M. I. Mech. E

*The Stanier Pacifics of the LMS* - Cecil J Allen

*Kings and Castles of the GWR* - O S Nock

*The McIntosh Locomotives* - A B MacLeod

*The Last Steam Locomotive Engineer, R A Riddles CBE* - Col. H C B Rogers OBE

*Southern Steam Surrender* - John H Bird

*The Lore of the Train* - C Hamilton Ellis

The pictures in this book were provided courtesy of the following:

GETTY IMAGES
101 Bayham Street, London NW1 0AG

MILEPOST 92 1/2T

LNWR COLLECTION

CLIVE GROOME'S PERSONAL COLLECTION

NATIONAL RAILWAY MUSEUM / SCIENCE
& SOCIETY PICTURE LIBRARY

Published by G2 Entertainment Limited

Publishers Jules Gammond and Alan Jones

Written by Clive Groome

With thanks to Mr Hardy for his kindness in checking the manuscript

To download our latest catalogue and to view
the full range of books and DVDs visit:

# www.G2ent.co.uk